Blended Learning & Flipped Classrooms: A Comprehensive Guide

Patricia Adams
Happy Gingras

First Edition

To order, contact:

The Part-Time Press

P.O. Box 130117

Ann Arbor, MI 48113-0117

Phone/Fax: 734-930-6854

First printing: December, 2017

© 2017 The Part-Time Press

ISBN: 978-0-940017-14-6 (paperback)

Printed in the United States of America

Table of Contents

Table of Figures

Preface

Welcome to the world of Flipped and Blended Learning! As your hosts for this journey, we would like to take a moment to thank you for choosing our book. This book is intended to be a guide and motivation for instructors, including adjunct instructors, to venture out of the lecture comfort zone and into the world of engaging pedagogy. Our book is a solid, basic guide for any college instructor wishing to explore this journey.

Every adventure has a beginning and our story is no different. We did not start with the intention of writing a book, consulting on course design, or giving speeches. However, that is exactly what has happened, and it still overwhelms us daily. We embarked on the journey into flipped and blended learning because it supported our goals as college teachers and advocates for our students. Apparently, when you embrace who you are and are true to your values and beliefs, opportunities present themselves.

We are full-time social science (psychology and sociology) instructors teaching in our respective disciplines and living in the isolated, siloed environment that is so easy to embrace in academia. It is far too easy to remain disconnected from your peers as an instructor since the nature of our work is so autonomous. We knew each other, had been to department meetings together, would even say hello in the hallways, but had never had any conversations of consequence. We barely knew anything about each other, with the exception of having good reputations as instructors on campus. What being a "good instructor" entailed was never clarified, but it was a reputation that we certainly didn't mind.

We had both been full-time instructors in the classroom for several years when we began to write this book, and had each spent several years as adjunct instructors before finding full-time appointments. We had been teaching just long enough to begin to feel competent, but also long enough to want more or risk facing the first stages of burnout. At the time, there were no movements on our campus to embrace new ideas or encourage experimentation. The general feeling was one of "If it ain't broke, why fix it?"

So, being relatively new kids on our respective blocks (with peers who had been teaching decades longer than we had) we went about our days relying mainly on lecture-based teaching with some active learning activities integrated.

Does this sound in any way like your own situation? Are you, like we were, searching for something to not only help your students learn, but also to invigorate your teaching and ignite your love for it?

The fact that we are book authors today is true serendipity. A change in leadership changed the dynamic in our department. While we were not initially encouraged to try different things, it was not actively discouraged either. A last minute cancellation by another instructor allowed us to be at the same conference together. The conference attendees were all psychology and sociology teachers from our home community college system, so we had a lot in common with them and wanted to connect with them. It was a relatively small but high quality conference that happened to be about flipped and active learning. As we attended the sessions together, we discussed the presenters' ideas, but little more. What we didn't know then was that we were both (inside our own heads) plotting and planning our own adventures into active learning.

After the conference ended, we waited in the lobby of the conference hotel while our department chair (and ride home) attended a meeting. This gave us about an hour to sit together, and so we sat down by the fireplace to chat about presenter, Porscha Orndorf. She had given a talk on flipping your classroom. We were both intrigued and excited about this idea, and started discussing how we were already using elements of flipping, but knew we could do so much more. It was actually surprising to find how much of the flipping process we were already using, which encouraged each of us to dive in.

As we talked by that roaring fire, we started to understand that we were kindred spirits. We were invested in our students' success and we were willing to take chances to make our courses more successful. Our shared ideas of flipping lessons turned into a discussion about how we could further flip our courses. Then, we took another step down the path and plotted a way to use the flipped classroom structure to give us enough class time to have our students collaborate on a project. Both of us had pens and paper out. It was a true frenzy of ideas.

Maybe it was a rebellion against having been siloed all of those years. Maybe it was a desire to bring the passion back into our teaching with something innovative. Whatever it was, it remains to this day one of the most intellectually stimulating and affirming conversations of our careers...and the most fortuitous.

We moved at lightning speed from an idea exchange to planning a joint research project that would combine the best elements from sociology with the best from psychology. This was the point at which we decided to take the biggest risk of our academic careers by designing a jointly taught flipped and blended course and implementing it the next semester (about eight weeks away at the time).

Even in our enthusiasm, we knew that we had to overcome major obstacles. We had to do an entire prep for a course in just a few weeks, and this prep had to be done jointly. However, we did not let these issues dissuade us from what had become our mission.

The only way to pull off the project was to totally flip our courses. As a result, we became quite skilled at flipping our classroom and employing technology to build a blended environment. We took stock of our strengths and what each of us brought to the table. One of us had a lot of contacts in administration and we decided to use those contacts to our advantage. The other one had in-depth knowledge of technological resources and excellent organizational skills. Together, we made it work. We hit the collaboration jackpot by finding each other and being so compatible as working partners.

This fireside chat was the beginning of many long nights, texts and emails. It was one of the most productive times of our academic careers. Yes, we worked hard — harder than we may have ever worked before — but it was energizing, fulfilling and scary. We created a project that represented each of our disciplines and radically changed how each of us was teaching our course materials.

Once the project was almost fully designed, we approached our department chair about instituting the changes we needed to make it work. The chair asked many, many questions and then gave a hesitant approval for us to try it in one set of classes. We were over the moon! We immediately made plans to start the project the next semester.

Our initial runs culminated in poster presentations by the students that we opened to the entire campus. To our joy and surprise, not only did many faculty, staff, and members of upper administration attend, but they were thrilled with the ideas that our student teams had developed. We received so much positive feedback and support from the administration that we moved to a "Shark Tank" design (complete with administrators acting as mentors and judges) for the next semester. Many of the ideas that our students created have been implemented, in part or as a whole, by the college. We had never anticipated the reaction that we got.

This story (and this book) is meant to inspire you, not to overwhelm you. We want to share with you what can be possible if you implement a flipped and blended course design to give yourself the face-to-face classroom time you need to employ more active learning strategies. We may have taken a dive into the deep end by doing it all at once, but that doesn't mean that you have to do the same. Instead, we want you to know that there are exciting possibilities out there waiting for you if you take a chance.

We urge you to consider flipping and blending your classes at whatever speed you are comfortable. If that means that you only flip one lesson, that is fine. In fact, it may be better to start slowly and add elements as you continue teaching. We flipped everything, and that led to a lot of planning, revising and thinking on the fly. It required flexibility and quick problem-solving skills at times too. However, this type of challenge stimulated us and infused our teaching with a passion that had been declining because we were not feeling challenged.

This journey started somewhat selfishly. We wanted to add some spice to our classes and to better engage our students in topics that interested us so much that we'd chosen to teach them for a living. What we got in return is hard to measure, though. We ended up with more work, but the intrinsic rewards have been well worth it.

We have now spent several years not only honing our own flipped and blended learning skills, but also working hard to share both the method and our own successes to motivate others. We consult with those who want to try flipped and blended learning both on campus and through conferences, workshops, and webinars. Now, we're going to share our love of flipped and blended learning with you. We hope you find this book useful, and that you find the joy that we have found in our own classrooms.

Before we let you get to the reading and course planning, we'd like to extend our heartfelt thanks to some very important people. First, to our families, who have put up with many late night text sessions, weekends away. We love you and thank you for your support. We want to thank our on-campus supporters, who are too numerous to name, but Sadie Oates, Stephanie Rook, Ayra Sundbom, Lori Preast and Angela Davis deserve special recognition. Tom Grady, our collaborator from afar, deserves our thanks as well for opening doors and helping us find more kindred spirits. Finally, to the North Carolina Community College Sociology and Psychology Association (NCCCSPA), we say thanks for the motivation and the fireside that sparked our life-changing chat.

Thanks, also, to you...our readers. We hope you find inspiration in our journey from Fireside Chats to Flipping over Flipping.

Patricia Adams and Happy Gingras

How To Get the Most Out of This Book

An important tool in this book is the use of icons to highlight important information for the reader.

Keys to Success: Whenever you see this icon, you'll want to take special note. These are tried and true tips, concepts and ideas to help you blend and flip your classes.

Caution Light: Whenever you see this icon, you'll know what others who have successfully blended and flipped their classes have discovered NOT to do while planning and teaching their courses.

In addition to the icons, the table of contents is very detailed to get you to the topic that most interests you at the moment. At the beginning of each chapter, you'll find boxes that will highlight important terms and ideas. An index has been compiled for ease of use. Finally, at the end of this book, there is a detailed section that deals with copyright guidelines for the college faculty member.

> **This book is your quick reference for blended and flipped teaching and learning. Use this book as a manual, a guide, or for professional reading. It contains practical and informative strategies to assist you. It is written in a user-friendly manner for your convenience. Enjoy it and GOOD TEACHING.**

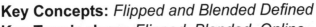
CHAPTER 1
WHAT IS FLIPPED & BLENDED LEARNING?

First things first…thanks for reading! If you've picked up this book, then you clearly care about your teaching and want the best for your students, and we're right there with you. No matter how much we wish, hope and look forward to having the perfect course filled with the perfect students, the stars never seem to align. Have you ever noticed that anytime college instructors get together to compare notes, the conversation inevitably circles around to faculty pet peeves and the students who commit them?

Here are several of the most common:

- Failing to come to class regularly;

- Arriving to class late (and especially making a big entrance), and worse, making a habit of it;

- Shuffling papers, putting books away, and other "end-of-class" behaviors before the class has ended;

- Questioning whether some of the homework for the class is just "busy work";

- Asking if "we're doing anything important in class";

- Asking what is happening in class when that information is in the syllabus;

- Allowing cell phones to ring in class;

- Texting in class;

- Holding a side discussion during class;

- Asking inane or off-topic questions;

- Eating in class;

- Claiming not to know an assignment was due, that there was a test, or any other class work that is clearly identified in the class calendar;

- Not completing the assigned reading before class;

- Sleeping during class;

- Complaining about the workload in class;

- Wearing inappropriate clothing (or the lack of it) to class;

- Asking to "borrow" a stapler to staple a homework assignment for the class;

- Turning in assignments that do not follow the assignment;

- Making excuses for missed exams, class assignments (Hansen, "College Professor Pet Peeves").

What would you say if we said you could avoid most of these by embarking on the journey into flipped and blended learning? Seem to good to be true? Well, it's not.

Randall Hansen, in his article "College Professor Pet Peeves and Positive Student Behaviors," not only gives us a list of pet peeves, but he also identifies positive behaviors that are common to students in flipped and blended learning environments. How would you like to see more of these behaviors from your students?

- Students take responsibility for their education;

- Students have read the assigned reading and actively participate in class discussion;

- Students complete all assigned work on time;

- Students sit toward the front of the classroom;

- Students visit professors during office hours;

- Students do not make excuses;

- Students ask for help more than a day before a test or an assignment due date.

Flipped and blended learning turns the traditional lecture classroom on its head and allows you to combine your own creativity with technological tools that help you use your classroom time more effectively and efficiently. As a result, your students are engaged, prepared, and often more excited about learning the course materials you are eager to provide and the teaching you are excited to do.

Before we dive into how to flip and blend your own courses, let's take a moment to understand flipped and blended learning and how it fits into the course platform options available to you when you're planning your courses.

If you could teach your course in such a way so as to actively engage every student, what would your course look like? What kinds of activities would you do in class, and what would you have the students do at home? How much technology would you introduce, if any? How would you be sure to cover all of the course materials by the end of the semester so that your students had opportunities to learn, practice and demonstrate critical thinking, analysis, and application skills?

Would a lecture-based course be able to accomplish all of those desired outcomes? Not really.

That's not to say that the lecture is outmoded or useless. On the contrary, lectures plays an important role in blended and flipped courses. The catch is that the lecture in a blended and flipped course is not delivered in the classroom, but rather out of class, where the student works independently. This flipping of the lecture means classroom time is available for active learning activities that lead to deeper student engagement.

As an instructor at a community college, I constantly strive to engage my students in the classroom environment. This can be a challenge at any academic level, but at the community college level it is particularly challenging considering the varied ages of our student population. For my students and I, flipping the classroom allows for the classroom to come alive with engagement and brings together a sense of community and connection

By Don King

Flipped Instruction

within the classroom like no other course platform I have ever used. A flipped classroom challenges students to be prepared for the lesson of the day and to work collaboratively and independently to communicate the information that traditionally would have been delivered via in-class lecture.

Flipping a classroom is a way to connect the multi-generational community college classroom with the course materials required for reading. This teaching method builds connections in a classroom and, in my experience, students adapt to this non-traditional teaching format very well. The flipped classroom is a way to foster confidence in both faculty and students, and bring a classroom alive though increased student engagement and interactivity. — *Don King, General Education Instructor, Pitt Community College, North Carolina*

We're going to be using specialized terms such as "blended," "hybrid," "traditional," "online," "virtual," "pedagogy" and "flipped" that may be a bit confusing to the uninitiated. If your degree is in adult education or you have a previous background in education, these terms may be familiar to you. However, most college instructors are hired because they are content experts. If this is the case with you, you may not have a working knowledge of these ideas. Don't worry. With a bit of effort, you'll be fluent in the necessary terminology in just a few minutes.

First, let's address one of the most commonly confused set of concepts first…course structure vs. pedagogy.

Structure	*Pedagogy*
Where (is the course taught)?	How (is the course taught)?
Classroom vs. hybrid/blended vs. internet	Lecture vs. flipped vs. active

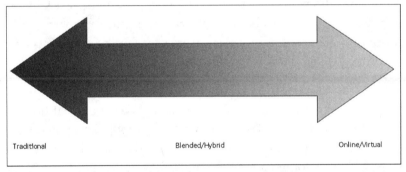

Figure 1.1: Continuum of the Structure of the Classroom

The majority of courses taught at colleges and universities today are structured in one of three ways: in a traditional classroom, online, using some combination of both.

There are several factors to consider when deciding how to structure your course; some of those may be determined in whole or part by the needs of your department or college. For example, there may be limited classroom space or a desire to offer a variety of course structures. It's important to understand the differences between the types of course structures before we move on.

Course Structures

Traditional Courses

In the traditional classroom structure, both the students and the instructor gather in a classroom for all of the contact hours of the course. It is a true, physical, face-to-face meeting. This course structure has, historically, been the most common structure of classes offered on college campuses. One of the main benefits of this course structure is, obviously, the contact and interaction between student and instructor. Instructors directly monitor student progress and struggles. The face-to-face traditional classroom course structure also allows intellectual exchange among the students and between the student and instructor, interactions that are more difficult to facilitate in online (virtual) learning environments. However, a student in a traditional classroom needs to have the time available to attend class meetings regularly, and must commit to scheduling other obligations, such as work and family, around the class meetings. This can prove to be difficult for some students, particularly those who are non-traditional students with family obligations and full or part-time jobs—a student demographic which is growing.

The development and expansion of educational technology have created many alternatives for course instruction that do not rely on the traditional classroom model. The popularity of online and hybrid courses has increased in over the past decade. Most colleges have adopted a learning management system, or LMS, to provide students and instructors with a place to share instructional information online. Common LMS options chosen by colleges and universities include Moodle, Blackboard, and Canvas. With the adoption of LMS technology, greater varieties of course structure options have become available to institutions (and instructors) to meet the needs of their diverse student populations.

Virtual Courses

One of those options is a fully online or virtual course. With online courses, all of the work is done without a required face-to-face meeting between the instructor and the student. There may be some synchronous (scheduled) meetings through formats such as Skype, webinar or video chat platforms, but the majority of students' work is completed asynchronously to provide flexibility to the student. Flexibility is a powerful benefit of this course structure, as is independence in learning. However, both the students and the instructor need a certain level of digital competency in order to effectively use this type of course structure. Students also need to be skilled in time management, and adept at self-motivation. Research shows that time management skills may be a more powerful predictor of a college freshman's GPA than SAT scores (Britton & Tesser, 1991; Thibodeaux, Deutsch, Kitsantas, & Winsler, 2016). Further, Thibodeaux et. al., 2016 found that students were more likely to lower their target GPA than increase their target study time goals when faced with a lower GPA than expected after their first semester of college. The issue of time management and self-motivation is even more critical in an online course than in a face-to-face setting.

Hybrid Courses

The final course structure blends both traditional classroom and online learning. Appropriately called blended or hybrid learning, it employs some combination of classroom meetings and online coursework. The percentage of time spent in the classroom versus online can vary widely. For example, one hybrid course may meet in person only for exams and practical assessments while another may meet 60-75 percent of the course contact hours in person. If envisioning course structure as a continuum with online at one extreme and traditional at the other, blended and hybrid learning encompasses everything between the extremes, and offers considerable flexibility in course structure. Just as with online courses, the student and the instructor need to have a certain level of digital proficiency in order to successfully take advantage of this type of classroom setting. However, this course structure allows the students and teacher to work together face-to-face in addition to the online requirements.

Which is the most effective course structure? There are certainly arguments for each of them, and challenges associated with each as well. Since you may not have a choice in your course structure, it's in the pedagogy that you will make the most of the structure that you have been given. Ideally, if you want to flip your course, you will make use of either a traditional or hybrid/blended course structure since the nature of the flipped course involves both face-to-face and out-of-class work to be completed by the student. However, a blended structure is optimal for a flipped classroom environment. Why? To understand we need to explain the differences between the pedagogical models.

Pedagogy

If traditional, blended and online are the structure options for courses, the options for how the course is taught would be called the pedagogy. The broad categories to be considered are these: lecture, active learning, and flipped.

Lecture

Who hasn't been on the receiving end of a lecture either in or outside of a classroom? The practice in the medieval university was for the instructor to read from an original source to a class of students who took notes on the lecture. Over the past 200 years, the diffusion of knowledge via handwritten lecture notes has been an essential element of academic life (Bligh, 2000). The lecture-based classroom pedagogy is familiar: during a lecture, information flows one way, from the instructor to the students. Students are expected to receive this information, take notes, and memorize. Students may be asked to apply the information learned, but that is usually done through projects and assignments completed outside of class meetings.

Lecture-based classrooms are led by the instructor who decides what is learned and when it is learned. A persistent criticism of lecture-based teaching and learning surrounds the passive nature of that pedagogical method. Numerous studies have concluded that lecturing is as effective, but not more effective, than any other teaching method used in transmitting information. Nevertheless, lecturing is not the most effective method for promoting student thought, changing attitudes, or teaching behavioral skills (Armstrong, and Scott, 2012).

Active Learning

Barnes, D. (1989) outlines the principles of active learning:

1. Purposive: the relevance of the task with the students' concerns.

2. Reflective: students' reflection on the meaning of what is learned.

3. Negotiated: negotiation of goals and methods of learning between students and teachers.

4. Critical: students appreciate different ways and means of learning the content.

5. Complex: students compare learning tasks with complexities existing in real life and making reflective analysis.

6. Situation Driven: the need of the situation is considered in order to establish learning tasks.

7. Engaged: real life tasks are reflected in the activities conducted for learning.

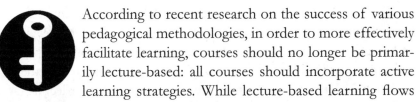 According to recent research on the success of various pedagogical methodologies, in order to more effectively facilitate learning, courses should no longer be primarily lecture-based: all courses should incorporate active learning strategies. While lecture-based learning flows from the instructor to the student, active learning facilitates a flow of information that is much more diverse. Adding active learning techniques to course delivery encourages questioning by the instructor and the students. Multiple pathways of communication help students grasp complex ideas and knowledge more efficiently. More importantly, the instructor who adopts active learning strategies will improve student retention and success. Incorporating activities such

as debates, games, minute-papers, think-pair-share, and others that will be discussed in detail later in this book, can increase student engagement and promote deeper learning.

The best evidence in favor of using active learning in the college classroom was provided by Dr. Benjamin Bloom, who authored Bloom's Taxonomy in 1956 (revised in 2001) (Anderson and Krathwohl, 2001).

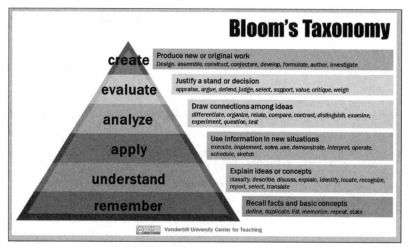

Figure 1.2: Bloom's Taxonomy

Bloom's Taxonomy shows the stages of learning and thinking beginning with lower levels of thinking and moving to higher levels of learning. In the traditional lecture-based classroom, for example, a teacher would guide students through the lowest two parts of the pyramid: understanding and remembering. The instructor lectures in the classroom and as the students take notes they begin to understand the course concepts. These notes then become the basis for memorization. After the lecture is finished, the instructor usually assigns some form of homework to help the students better understand the information they received in lecture.

In an active learning classroom environment, however, students engage the material at the higher levels of Bloom's taxonomy: they analyze, apply and create, reaching a higher level of learning. Active learning activities offer students the opportunity to apply their learning in order to gain skills that are transferable to the workplace such as critical thinking, collaboration, and presentation.

Flipped Classroom

We have established that the lecture-based classroom is a passive learning environment, and the active learning classroom is more interactive. When deeper learning is the course objective, as it is an active learning environment, how does an instructor make sure the students have a fundamental understanding of the more basic course concepts? After all, students can't apply, analyze, or create without a solid knowledge base. As seen in Figure 1.2, you need to cover the lower levels of the pyramid in order to reach the higher levels. If you jump straight into the active learning without creating the requisite solid foundation, academically unprepared and underprepared students may view your course as "too hard" and they'll drop the class. In other words, student retention will suffer.

At its most basic level, the flipped classroom sends the lecture home and brings the homework into class. Students master the remembering and understanding of general course information (vocabulary, concepts, etc.) through individual activities outside of class, demonstrate their mastery and receive any remediation needed, and then move into the classroom for active learning strategies that tap into higher levels of learning. The flipped classroom uses both lecture and active learning, but uses them in a "flipped" way. By moving the instruction of course materials related to the bottom levels of Bloom's pyramid out of the classroom, time is freed up in the classroom. That time is used to build upon the basic knowledge learned by students independently and this allows you and your students to focus in class time on activities related to the upper levels of Bloom's knowledge and learning pyramid.

One of the most important differences between an active learning traditional classroom and a flipped classroom is that the students are responsible for bringing a certain level of knowledge to a flipped classroom acquired by completing required out-of-class coursework. Flipped learning pedagogy is, essentially, the reverse of the lecture-based classroom. Homework is done in class and lectures are completed as homework.

As each type of pedagogy has strengths and weaknesses, instructors need to be mindful of course content in order to engage students most effectively. This means that where and how you teach require conscious consideration of your students, their academic needs and challenges, your course goals and your own areas of technological and academic expertise.

Why Flip and Blend?

It's advantageous to both the instructor and the students to combine blended and flipped learning:

- Blended course structures involve a mixture of classroom and internet learning.

- Blended courses allow an instructor the freedom to make the "flipped" course work much more interactive, including recorded lectures and assigned videos.

- Blended courses, with their integration of technology and multi-media tools outside of the classroom, provide opportunities to use active learning strategies both in class and at home.

- Flipped learning requires that students gain mastery of the remembering and understanding levels of Bloom's pyramid out of class. In class the focus is on activities that target learning at *higher levels of Bloom's pyramid*.

Keep in mind that to truly gain mastery of the basic knowledge of any assigned topic, a student must interact with it. At the very minimum, textbook reading and video watching will work in a blended and flipped course, but incorporating resources that can, for example, present questions intermittently within a video to measure comprehension or provide an interactive game environment to test vocabulary, will improve student engagement.

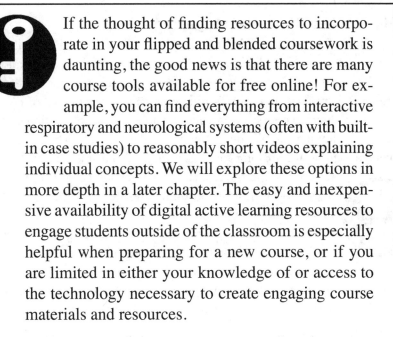

If the thought of finding resources to incorporate in your flipped and blended coursework is daunting, the good news is that there are many course tools available for free online! For example, you can find everything from interactive respiratory and neurological systems (often with built-in case studies) to reasonably short videos explaining individual concepts. We will explore these options in more depth in a later chapter. The easy and inexpensive availability of digital active learning resources to engage students outside of the classroom is especially helpful when preparing for a new course, or if you are limited in either your knowledge of or access to the technology necessary to create engaging course materials and resources.

Always investigate online resources before reinventing the wheel. Be sure you understand copyright and fair use rules before you incorporate materials found online into your courses.

A flipped classroom allows students to focus on tasks related to remembering and understanding—the lower levels of thinking on Bloom's pyramid—outside of the classroom. They can do this work without the use of technology. For instance, you can ask students to take notes on reading assignments and submitting the notes in class. There are as many ways to help students understand and remember information when working independently outside the classroom as there are types of information to remember. We will discuss a number of options in detail later. However, combining flipped learning with a blended course structure, you will have the freedom to leverage technology to make your students' out-of-class work more interactive and engaging.

More Active Student Engagement

Think for a moment. Why were you excited to make your academic discipline your life's work? Students in your classes should be just as excited about your discipline as you are! In order to keep students from dropping courses and, potentially, dropping out of college, introductory courses you teach must be engaging, exciting and relevant. Flipping and blending your courses allows you to be creative when designing and shaping your assignments. Your students will better understand the relevance of your subject area to their lives and be more profoundly engaged with the subject matter. Students who are engaged with the course material have better classroom and individual performances (higher grades, more time on task, etc.). Research consistently finds this to be true regardless of the discipline or subject being taught or the setting of the learning (Newman, Wehledge, Lamborn, 1992; Klem & Connell, 2004; Zepke & Leach, 2010).

Active engagement leads to increased participation in class discussions, which is a gauge that instructors often used to measure the level of a student's participation. (Grieve & Lesko, 2011).

Data Driven Classroom Instruction

It is important to make sure that the students are completing out-of-class work. This is one of the key instructor tasks in a flipped classroom. In order to do this, a blended course structure uses technology. Technology allows for easier measures of student mastery without taking time away from in-class active learning.

For example, a student can complete an assignment through an adaptive quizzing program provided by your textbook publisher. Such tools provide the instructor with data on student performance and mastery which should, in turn, drive in-class activities and determine areas of particular instructional need. Blending and flipping takes much of the guess work out of whether students are achieving appropriate and expected levels of subject matter mastery.

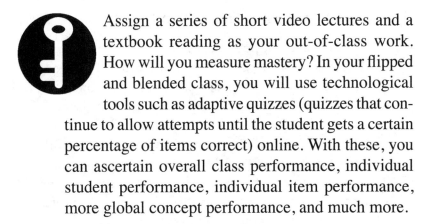 Assign a series of short video lectures and a textbook reading as your out-of-class work. How will you measure mastery? In your flipped and blended class, you will use technological tools such as adaptive quizzes (quizzes that continue to allow attempts until the student gets a certain percentage of items correct) online. With these, you can ascertain overall class performance, individual student performance, individual item performance, more global concept performance, and much more.

In the blended and flipped classroom, data let you know when your students are ready to move into the application and analysis phases of learning (see Bloom's pyramid). Data also let you know whether they need remediation before moving forward. The use of technology within the blended course structure makes such decisions much more straight forward.

An End to the Sage on the Stage

Can you imagine having to research answers to student questions because your students are reaching such advanced levels of inquiry? This can and does routinely happen in flipped and blended classrooms!

The very best advantage that we have found as instructors in flipped and blended classrooms is that the instructor is no longer "sage on the stage" who simply lectures to students. In flipped and blended classrooms, we are working with students and listening to them. Meanwhile, students are reaching the higher levels of thinking and reasoning shown in Bloom's Taxonomy.

Flipped and blended learning helps students effectively enter the higher levels of learning, and gain the critical thinking, analysis and synthesis skills they need to succeed in college, and in the transition from college to the workplace. Students practice their soft skills through interactions with you, the course materials and with each other.

Even More Reasons to Flip & Blend

- **In blended and flipped classrooms, the instructor is *not* the hardest-working person in the room.** If you are giving a lecture, you are the hardest-working person in the room. Think about that. All the pressure is on the lecturer to perform and provide, while students passively absorb what the instructor delivers. However, when students work toward being more responsible for their own educations, they assume more of the workload. By engaging your students with learning activities that allow them to create, analyze, and evaluate, you are putting your students to work. *Remember, students who are engaged are more likely to stay in your class and in college.*

- **Today's students are extremely comfortable using technology**, even if they are "digital immigrants" instead of "digital natives." Since technology plays such a large role in our personal and professional lives, it is important that graduates from our colleges are comfortable with the use of technology in a variety of scenarios (not just texting or social media use, for example). Therefore, incorporating multi-media and technology into our classrooms and course materials makes good sense.

- **Blending and flipping will save you time.** Think about the prep that you need to do for a lecture-based class. Whether you have a 50 minute, 90 minute, or three-hour class, it requires preparation to deliver a lecture. Each time you teach a particular course, you need to review, revise and update your lecture notes. If you blend and flip your classroom, you will also need to create course materials, but the materials are different in a blended and flipped class. You can expect to create worksheets, short lectures and write-ups, among other materials. Once you have created the infrastructure for your course, you are well on your way to repurposing your time toward making it better every semester. You will be able to make your overall course content stronger and to do so more quickly.

- **Blending and flipping your classroom will allow your students to comprehend the connections between different topics more readily (deeper thinking).** Connections between concepts are often difficult for new college students to find on their own. Blending and flipping provides opportunities to help students move along the path to creative and evaluative (higher) learning. They (and you) will experience the benefits of moving beyond the basic knowledge level of the course.

- **Using flipped and blended active learning allows students to sharpen the soft skills that employers value.** These skills include the ability to listen to others and summarize what they have to say, to present information professionally and to disagree appropriately by using relevant research. These are essential skills in virtually any workplace.

To help your students master these so-called soft skills, have them create presentations, portfolios and brochures.

If you want your students to be higher order learners, want them to take ownership of their learning and you want to experience better student (and instructor) engagement, then flipped and blended teaching and learning are definitely for you.

We each jumped into flipped and blended teaching and learning from the high dive; we flipped and blended *all* of our courses. While you're certainly free to do that, remember that you don't have to flip and blend all of your courses in a single semester or even a single year. As you realize time savings, you can migrate course materials and courses to this platform. While you read this book, think about a lesson or module that you can flip and how you would then blend that lesson.

If you need any added incentive to flip and blended your courses, remember those positive student behaviors we discussed at the beginning of this chapter. You will absolutely see those in your flipped and blended classrooms, just as we have.

Key Concept: *Mindset*
Key Idea: *Flipped instruction can take many different forms. It must be relevant, engaging and appropriately measure learning.*

CHAPTER 2
LETTING GO OF THE LECTURE

We hope you are starting to get excited about blending and flipping a course or two. There is an important discussion we need to have before moving on to the mechanics of blending and flipping. We want you to take an honest look at—and prepare to change—your mindset about "the lecture" as a primary pedagogical strategy.

You Are No Longer the "Sage on the Stage"

It is very likely that you sat in many lecture-based courses as a college student. Since this pedagogical strategy is familiar, it is often the pedagogy instructors gravitate toward when planning and designing a course. A lecture requires the instructor to provide information and puts students in the role of passive recipients of that information. It is easy to get accustomed to the expectation that you will "feed" your students the course materials and assume full responsibility for student learning. In the blended and flipped classroom, lecture-based instruction is replaced by a two-way communication flow between student and teacher.

Let go of the lecture? You may find yourself wondering how you will cover all of the course materials. However, you will read in this chapter why today's college students do not find lectured-based instruction to be the most effective way to learn and in subsequent chapters exactly how you will cover the course materials. When you blend and flip your classroom, you place more of the responsibility for their own learning on the students. Flipping and blending

L ike most instructors, I have been lecturing rather than focusing on active learning strategies to engage my students. Lecturing fit my personality. I covered all the topics I felt were pertinent. To highlight topics, I told stories that connected ideas to the "real world." That being said, lecturing was tedious and it was sometimes boring to repeat information in the same way year after year.

By Jean Cahoon
Flipped Instruction

I had the opportunity to sit in on a colleague's night class and participate in a flipped activity. The students were excited and engaged, and I was hooked on flipped learning. I started attending professional development presentations on how to flip a class and did research on active, brain-based learning.

Sifting through course materials and deciding on which topics to transform can be a challenge. Each semester I tweak my flipped learning activities, add new ones or scrap activities that did not work. My teaching does not seem stale anymore, because it's always evolving. My students and I learn new ways of learning information that is critical to the curriculum, yet exciting to learn. — *Jean Cahoon, Psychology Instructor, Pitt Community College, Adjunct Psychology Instructor, East Carolina University, North Carolina* changes the information pathway from one-way (instructor to student) into a multi-directional flow of information. This improved flow is what leads to students learning the basics prior to in-class work. During class time, rather than listen to you lecture about the materials, students make use of the time with you to engage with the course materials more actively and deeply.

We understand that it is hard to let go of the idea that you are the best (and often only) source of information that the students have for your course. Where else will they get the information if not from you? Isn't it your job to give it to them?

In reality, students have a variety of resources for every course they take: textbooks, Google, YouTube and other options exist in a range of formats to effectively meet the needs of the learner. Will they take advantage of those resources? Flipped and blended learning motivates students (Bhagat, et. al., 2016). A motivated student will learn about a topic whether you lecture on that topic or not.

This should not be understood to mean that in blended and flipped courses we never lecture. We do. Lecture has a place and is used in the blended and flipped course. How a lecture is structured is quite different, however. The majority of the lectures you'll prepare will be "mini-lectures," usually only about 5-10 minutes long. Your lectures will focus on specific information and a single topic in the course.

Use mini-lectures to record quick talks on specific points in a chapter/topic and upload the mini-lectures to the course Learning Management System (LMS) so that students can listen at home. Technical jargon and vocabulary are always good mini-lectures. Focus mini-lectures on course concepts that students struggle to understand. If you have a favorite story that illustrates course content, make a mini-lecture. Any small chunk of course content can become a mini-lecture.

The key with these recorded mini-lectures is to aim for no more than a five-minute talk. Why five minutes? Pretend you are seeking information about a home improvement job. You decide to look at YouTube videos. Your search brings up videos that are that are 60, 30, 20 and 5 minutes long. Which do you pick to watch? Most people will start with the five minute video and then watch other videos or seek out more information if they want to learn more.

"Over the last year and a half, according to the numbers compiled by ComScore, the amount of video Americans watch online has stayed pretty steady, but the length of each individual video has reversed its rise and has plummeted over the last year from nearly 7 minutes to just over 5 minutes" (Greenfield, 2013).

Give students a snippet of information to get them intrigued. Then, in class, you will follow that up with active learning activities. Student engagement will soar.

You will also use mini-lectures in the classroom. A major advantage of the blended and flipped classroom is that you will benefit from the multi-directional flow of information, so you can more easily gauge student comprehension and use mini-lectures to deepen learning. As your blended and flipped course progresses, expect students to give more input than they would in a lecture course format. As the students give input, stay alert to concepts and information the students may not have grasped fully. "Muddy points" for one student are likely to be problematic for multiple students. When you identify a muddy point, use a mini-lecture to clarify it, and then assess student mastery before moving on. Such adjustments can only happen in a classroom that is flexible.

In vs. Out

Letting go of the lecture means when designing and planning your course you will need to identify which course content to cover in the classroom and which content students should cover outside of class. There are several considerations to think about when making these decisions.

Since this class should be fun for you, consider what you like to teach. Focus on these topics in the classroom. Your passion will come through, and students will pick up on that. You will be a more dynamic facilitator.

For work that requires memorization, create flash cards or guided notes. Take the textbook publisher's PowerPoint slides and remove some of the information. Students work to complete the slides.

As we all have topics about which we are passionate, we also have topics that challenge us or are more difficult to teach. This should weigh in your decision to make it an in-class lesson or not. Being less excited about a topic can make it difficult to lead an active learning session on it. These are topics that you might want to consider making mainly out of class work. However, be sure that you create appropriate resources for this learning to allow students to engage with the material.

A third important consideration for deciding which course materials to keep in the classroom is to isolate the topics with which students are most likely to struggle. These topics should always be addressed in the classroom setting so you can measure understanding through your interactions with the students. If this is your first time teaching a particular course, identifying these tricky topics can be harder, but your peers are an excellent resource to point you in the right direction.

Scaffold lessons so that students have the support they need to gain basic understanding of the topic. Creating a pre-lesson to be completed outside of the classroom will prepare students for higher levels of learning when they get to class.

Determine where the various course content falls within Bloom's Taxonomy. If the materials focus is a lower level of thinking and learning, such as memorization or comprehension, then these materials can be completed by your students outside of the classroom. The skill level of your students will determine the level of support or scaffolding your students require. If you have underprepared students, they will require more support.

 To help students with comprehension outside of the classroom, a large quiz bank can be useful. You can allow multiple attempts to allow for learning and grade for mastery.

Course content that requires application and analysis are appropriate for an in-class assignment, but there are times when they can be completed outside of the classroom provided you put in place proper supports, such as a rubric or in-class tutorials.

Learning activities and course content that require evaluation and creation should be done in the classroom.

 Application and analysis skills (problem-based learning) can be practiced with case studies, videos and presentations.

Selling Flipped to Your Students

If stakeholders are not supportive of your efforts to innovate. Even the most meticulously prepared blended and flipped course can fail to meet course objectives and educational goals. This means that you need to get the students you teach on board.

One way to introduce the idea of a flipped classroom is by presenting the following scenario to the students:

"Have you ever had a class where the teacher lectures the whole time? Then the teacher gives you a homework assignment where you are expected to apply and create something based on the lecture? Have you ever gotten home and not understood the assignment, been frustrated and had no one to ask about it? What if we flipped this around in this classroom?"

Then, show your students Bloom's Taxonomy and talk about the different levels of learning. Explain how a flipped class can reduce student frustration and failure. Ask for a vote: "Who wants a lecture based course and who wants a flipped course?" In our own courses, we have always had unanimous votes for a flipped course.

 Fortunately, selling the concept of a blended and flipped class to students is generally not difficult. The one thing that is of critical importance is that you clearly articulate the expectations of the blended and flipped course. Most students are receptive to a course structure in which they have a chance to actively engage and to have their voices heard.

There are specific expectations for the learners. Students must understand that they need to complete the required out-of-class assignments or they will face consequences. These consequences may be a pop quiz, no participation points, or whatever suits the instructor and the class situation. Sometimes the consequence is a natural one, i.e. they cannot participate in the in-class activity their outside work would have prepared them to do. Students need to be held accountable so that they come to class prepared and ready to engage with the material. Once the prepared student is in the classroom, the next expectation is that the student will be an active participant in the course.

As an instructor in a blended and flipped classroom, remember that this level of active participation could be an entirely new skill set for these students to master. You may need to scaffold this learning by providing more support until the students gain the confidence and skills needed to become more active participants in their learning experience.

 Ask more prompting questions during a class discussion at the beginning of the semester than at the end of the semester. Provide worksheets to help students complete their reading, or guided notes to help them identify the important topics.

To sell blended and flipped to your students, explain what you are bringing to the table, what their expectations of you can be. As instructors, we have responsibilities to our students. We begin our commitment to a course by creating a plan in which the chapter or unit learning objectives support the course learning objectives, and by creating activities that support both of these important educational goals. We create meaningful learning sessions. Communicate this to your students, the learners, so that they understand that as the instructor you are equally invested in the course.

Just as we ask our students to bring their best to our classroom, we must hold ourselves accountable to do the same. By helping the students understand what they can expect of you in the classroom, it becomes easier for all participants to comprehend that this is a group effort. The class will only improve if everyone commits to putting forth their best effort and keeping an open mind.

Staying Connected

Cartoonstock.com

Letting go of the lecture and using a flipped classroom means developing more connections. There are four main constituencies with whom you need to maintain connections: students, your co-workers, like-minded instructors of any discipline who teach flipped and blended courses, and any outside/online groups and resources.

Student Connections

Student connections tend to be easy to create and maintain because of the nature of how the course is managed. Instead of lecturing to a sea of bored faces, you are interacting with students individually or in small groups. You'll create meaningful interactions and connections with all of your students. These connections will help to lead to better retention, students with stronger soft skills and greater enthusiasm.

You'll know you have connected with your students when they send a random email with a link to a resource that might be good to use in class, or when they share a story about how they experienced something that they learned in class. These connections will result in profound, meaningful teaching and learning experiences.

Instructor Connections

Along with the students, it is always good to maintain connections with the other instructors in your discipline. They may be people at your home institution, at other institutions or even in an online group. It is wonderful to have a group you can share ideas and resources with. These connections can help not only with course content, but also with other classroom issues you might be experiencing. In addition, if you are connected with the full time instructors in your area, you are more likely to be kept abreast of changes and policies that may affect you.

Finding other like-minded "flippers" is another great connection to have. As you move into flipping, it is likely that you realize that you have already been doing some lessons that are flipped. Taking that next step into flipping can be a bit scary. Talking to other people who are familiar with this teaching style can help you to feel less alone. They can also help you to troubleshoot any issues you might be having. Every time that we a "flipping" training at a college, we hear from the attendees that getting a chance to work with others who flip helps to make them feel as though they have a support system and it makes them feel less alone. When you are teaching in a blended and flipped classroom, it makes even more sense to collaborate with others.

We have found that discipline does not matter when collaborating with other "flippers." The processes of flipping work are the same in all disciplines, so that talking to others about what they do in class can give you some great ideas. You might be able to take a website, idea, or activity and change it to meet the goals of your course. Or you could ask for idea about how to approach a topic.

Bringing different disciplines together to brainstorm creates some amazing, unique ideas!

Finally, you want to stay connected to any outside groups you can join. Your professional association may have a list of resources available for members. They may also have chat rooms or blogs with classroom ideas. Facebook has many different teaching groups that share information. There are many teaching blogs you can subscribe to. AdjunctNation.com, *The Chronicle of Higher Education* and other teaching journals have websites that have articles, information and forums that can be helpful.

All of these are great sources of support and allow you to engage at some level with other professionals. However, you should be constantly looking online yourself for resources, ideas and other things that will be useful to your course. There are many interactive websites, videos and worksheet ideas to be found for free on the internet. We give you more ideas in the next few chapters to help you scour the web for resources that work for you.

We hope that you are getting excited about flipping and blending your classroom. Hopefully, this and the other chapters you have read are getting your creative juices flowing. Now it is time to move into some of the hard-core thinking about exactly what you are going to do with your class. Follow us as we move into the planning stage of this process.

> **Key Concepts:** *Get to know your students.*
> **Key Terminology:** *Gen X, Gen Y, Gen Z, Traditionalists, Boomers, Digital Native, Digital Immigrant*
> **Key Idea:** *Student diversity shapes teaching.*

CHAPTER 3
WHO IS SITTING IN YOUR CLASSROOM?

As you ponder what you'll do with a semester-long course, your mind probably drifts back to your time in college lecture halls and classrooms. How many hours did you spend listening to the "sage on the stage" while scribbling notes? How much time did you spend reviewing those notes, completing study guides and memorizing facts and figures in order to earn your degrees?

Now you are a professional with valuable knowledge gained through experience and your own education. You may be tempted to teach your course the way you were taught. That is where most novice instructors look for inspiration. There's just one problem: your students.

How long ago did you earn your highest degree? Perhaps you have spent a decade working in your chosen field. Perhaps you graduated last year, and are still adjusting to post-graduate life. Even the most recent graduates of advanced degree programs experienced different learning environments as undergraduates than they are likely to face as faculty members.

A new generation has started college and is taking classes alongside an increasing number of older students returning to college after time in the workforce. There is also a growing number of first generation college students. College enrollment has become more diverse than ever before, with greater gender, age, racial and socioeconomic variability.

The expectations and views of education held by many of today's college students are drastically different from those of previous generations. Students enrolled in colleges across the country expect that they will be afforded more flexibility as they pursue their educational goals and that the mode of instruction will go beyond the traditional lecture as the sole mode of instruction.

By Tom Grady
Flipped Instruction

This trend extends beyond traditional college students and includes an increasing number of non-traditional students. According to the 2016 New Media Consortium Horizon Report, both millennials and a majority of nontraditional college students are demanding greater flexibility and delivery models which leverage technology to foster ubiquitous access to learning experiences.

Blended and flipped learning environments are two approaches to course design and pedagogy that are learner-centered and can lead to improved levels of student success. The two approaches offer the flexibility that many students are looking for and expecting when they arrive on our campuses.

Courses that are designed using a flipped or blended approach offer the opportunity for faculty to implement high impact, active learning experiences in the classroom. The traditional lecture method will always have a place in education. However, faculty are now expected to design courses and learning experiences that deviate from passive learning and place a greater emphasis on active learning. As a result, these two approaches should be strongly considered.

So what does all of this mean for higher education faculty? Quite simply all faculty at our nation's colleges and universities should strive to design their courses so that they incorporate innovative and high impact practices (focus on active and student-centered learning).

With this being said, students are still responsible for taking ownership of their education and learning. The shift in higher education is to create educational environments that focus on learner-centered teaching to increase student success.

Right, wrong or indifferent, and whether or not faculty agree with this approach, this is what today's college students expect. As faculty we must strive to learn more about our students so that we can increase levels of learner engagement on our campuses and in our classrooms.—*Tom Grady, Faculty Assistant Director, Center for Teaching Excellence, Kansas City Kansas Community College, Kansas.*

Add to this the fact that a greater number of students are facing challenges (both visible and invisible) that make college a very different experience: mental health challenges, learning disabilities, and other potential barriers are a more pervasive part of college life than you may have seen before. For instance, between .7 percent and 1.9 percent of college students could meet criteria for High Functioning Autism Spectrum Disorder (White, Olenick and Bray, 2011). According to a 2013 American Psychological Association survey, about one-third of college students have experienced depression within the past year and had difficulty functioning because of it (Novotney, 2014).

What could this mean for you and your course plans? To answer that question, let's take a closer look at the modern student and see who may be sitting in your classroom.

College enrollment has increased dramatically in the past decade. However, few demographic groups of students have increased as quickly as first generation college students. Researchers estimate that as many as 30 percent of today's college students are the first in their families to attend college (Opidee, 2015). The first generation student faces a "myriad of challenges in pursuit of earning college degrees (Hsiao, 1992; Mitchell, 1997)." These challenges include straddling two worlds. One world exists on the college campus, where these students are expected to be without the support of previous college graduates at home. The other world exists at home, where higher education may or may not be valued, but where responsibilities and expectations related to college homework and schedules do not have prior experience on which to be based.

Poverty is another significant challenge facing the first generation. An estimated 24 percent of current college students are both first generation and low-income (Opidee, 2015). That means that nearly one-quarter of your students may be at high risk for dropping out before they even step into a classroom, and face challenges that have little to do with the course material you plan to cover. You may be teaching students who are housing and food insecure. With such basic needs unmet can they focus as well as your other students?

Student Diversity

College campuses are becoming more ethnically diverse than ever. The U.S. Census Bureau estimates that by 2050, over half of the students enrolled in U.S. colleges and universities will come from groups that are currently classified as "minorities." This can be partially attributed to the current economic climate, supportive legislation for higher education, and increasing high school graduation rates (Association of American Colleges and Universities, 2010). Here is an overview of student ethnicity as of the fall of 2014 from the National Center for Educational Statistics:

Student Ethnicity

Level of enrollment and race/ethnicity of student	Total, all institutions	Public institutions	4-year							2-year	Total
		Total	Total	Research university, very high[1]	Research university, high[2]	Doctoral/research university[3]	Master's[4]	Bacca-laureate[5]	Special focus[6]		
1	2	3	4	5	6	7	8	9	10	11	12
											Fall enrollment
All students, total	20,375,789	14,745,558	8,120,417	2,363,477	1,478,612	416,284	2,655,967	1,115,474	90,603	6,625,141	3,974,004
White	11,590,717	8,364,146	4,866,761	1,428,602	927,266	244,641	1,594,482	619,767	52,003	3,497,385	2,475,173
Black	2,872,126	1,886,791	908,928	148,717	147,203	95,666	340,453	169,167	7,722	977,863	488,747
Hispanic	3,091,112	2,477,489	1,063,611	234,598	184,106	39,179	380,456	218,347	6,925	1,413,878	354,386
Asian	1,198,545	905,582	526,178	236,360	73,773	10,520	151,617	43,442	10,466	379,404	239,549
Pacific Islander	61,053	39,171	18,564	4,762	2,699	416	5,840	4,746	101	20,607	9,953
American Indian/Alaska Native	162,563	124,615	58,119	10,140	10,575	1,622	19,267	9,047	7,468	66,496	21,726
Two or more races	559,362	413,354	233,403	75,703	41,301	9,768	74,831	29,736	2,064	179,951	101,284
Nonresident alien	840,311	534,410	444,853	224,595	91,689	14,472	89,021	21,222	3,854	89,557	283,186
Undergraduate	17,474,835	13,347,002	6,721,861	1,782,454	1,175,173	335,829	2,289,498	1,106,290	32,617	6,625,141	2,757,447
White	9,899,168	7,522,236	4,024,851	1,091,635	738,885	198,244	1,365,163	613,472	17,452	3,497,385	1,755,481
Black	2,504,814	1,758,975	781,112	116,931	123,506	79,191	290,640	168,029	2,815	977,863	350,822
Hispanic	2,870,150	2,369,192	955,314	198,609	160,635	32,936	343,080	217,789	2,265	1,413,878	266,438
Asian	1,010,138	820,653	441,249	194,586	60,059	8,010	133,971	42,962	1,661	379,404	147,827
Pacific Islander	54,221	37,137	16,530	3,840	2,282	353	5,295	4,704	56	20,607	7,062
American Indian/Alaska Native	147,766	117,277	50,781	7,610	8,927	1,301	16,655	8,993	7,140	66,496	16,680
Two or more races	505,174	387,393	207,442	64,184	36,066	8,487	68,340	29,504	861	179,951	78,758
Nonresident alien	483,404	334,139	244,582	105,059	44,813	7,307	66,199	20,837	367	89,557	134,379
Postbaccalaureate	2,900,954	1,398,556	1,398,556	581,023	303,439	80,455	366,469	9,184	57,986	†	1,216,557
White	1,691,549	841,910	841,910	336,967	188,381	46,397	229,319	6,295	34,551	†	719,692
Black	367,312	127,816	127,816	31,786	23,697	16,475	49,813	1,138	4,907	†	137,925
Hispanic	220,962	108,297	108,297	35,989	23,471	6,243	37,376	558	4,660	†	87,948
Asian	188,407	84,929	84,929	41,774	13,714	2,510	17,646	480	8,805	†	91,722
Pacific Islander	6,832	2,034	2,034	922	417	63	545	42	45	†	2,891
American Indian/Alaska Native	14,797	7,338	7,338	2,530	1,648	321	2,457	54	328	†	5,046
Two or more races	54,188	25,961	25,961	11,519	5,235	1,281	6,491	232	1,203	†	22,526
Nonresident alien	356,907	200,271	200,271	119,536	46,876	7,165	22,822	385	3,487	†	148,807

Figure 3.1: U.S. resident undergraduate enrollment in degree-granting postsecondary institutions, by institutional level and control and student race/ethnicity: Fall 2014. **NOTE**: Degree-granting institutions grant associate's or higher degrees and participate in Title IV federal financial aid programs. Race categories exclude persons of Hispanic ethnicity. Detail may not sum to totals because of rounding. SOURCE: U.S. Department of Education, National Center for Education Statistics, Integrated Postsecondary Education Data System (IPEDS), Spring 2014, Enrollment component. See Digest of Education Statistics 2014, table 306.50.

Traditional vs. Non-Traditional Students

College populations, whether at a two-year, four-year, or other types of academic institutions, are often referred to as "traditional" or "nontraditional" based on student age. Traditional students are generally those age 25 or younger and nontraditional students are those who are age 26 or older. According to the National Center for Education Statistics, we are seeing an ever-increasing number of nontraditional students in the classroom. Depending on the type of institution, you may find that the "traditional" college student (under age 25) may be a minority in your classroom. Below is a snapshot of student ages from Fall 2015:

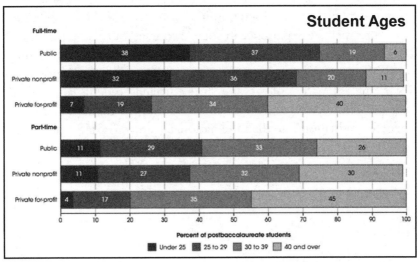

Figure 3.2: Percentage of full-time and part-time postbaccalaureate enrollment in degree-granting postsecondary institutions, by institutional control and student age: Fall 2015. **NOTE**: Degree-granting institutions grant associate's or higher degrees and participate in Title IV federal financial aid programs. Detail may not sum to totals because of rounding and the exclusion of students whose age was unknown. SOURCE: U.S. Department of Education, National Center for Education Statistics, Integrated Postsecondary Education Data System (IPEDS), Spring 2016, Fall Enrollment component. See Digest of Education Statistics 2016, table 303.50.

As of 2016, a new generation not only entered college, but now makes up a significant portion of the "traditional" cohort of students. "Generation Z," also called iGen, are as young as 4-5 years old, and as old college undergrads, depending on the source used to define this generation's age brackets (Barnes and Noble College, 2016; McCrindle, 2015). Unlike Baby Boomers and Gen Xers, Generation Z students who are still in high school now have the opportunity to take college courses, thanks to wide-reaching initiatives such as dual enrollment and early college high school. Dual enrollment enables high school students, usually those with high levels of achievement, to take college courses while earning their high school diplomas. Early college high school provides students with opportunities to earn both a high school diploma and an associate's degree simultaneously. The Early College Initiative started in 2002, thanks in part to the Bill and Melinda Gates Foundation, and now serves more than 50,000 students in 28 states (Webb & Mayka, 2011). Early college and dual enrolled students bring not only a new generation into your college classroom who may already have experience in college courses, but also represent a cohort of students who are not yet legally adults and who may not have the maturity some of your non-traditional students possess. Nonetheless, early college and dual enrolled students also bring unique perspectives and experiences, and have a higher bachelor's degree graduation rate than the national average (ESHS Initiative).

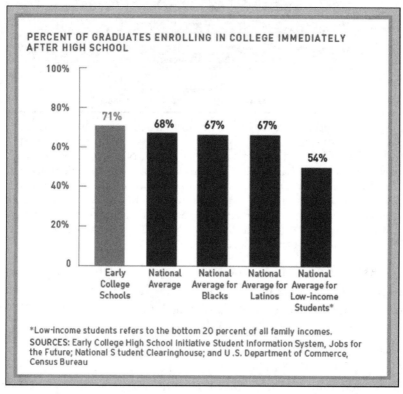

Figure 3.3: Percent of graduates enrolling after high school.

Chart 1: An overview of the working generations					
Characteristics	Maturists (pre-1945)	Baby Boomers (1945-1960)	Generation X (1961-1980)	Generation Y (1981-1995)	Generation Z (Born after 1995)
Formative experiences	Second World War, Rationing, Fixed-gender roles, Rock 'n' Roll, Nuclear families, Defined gender roles — particularly for women	Cold War, Post-War boom, "Swinging Sixties", Apollo Moon landings, Youth culture, Woodstock, Family-orientated, Rise of the teenager	End of Cold War, Fall of Berlin Wall, Reagan / Gorbachev, Thatcherism, Live Aid, Introduction of first PC, Early mobile technology, Latch-key kids; rising levels of divorce	9/11 terrorist attacks, PlayStation, Social media, Invasion of Iraq, Reality TV, Google Earth, Glastonbury	Economic downturn, Global warming, Global focus, Mobile devices, Energy crisis, Arab Spring, Produce own media, Cloud computing, Wiki-leaks
Percentage in U.K. workforce*	3%	33%	35%	29%	Currently employed in either part-time jobs or new apprenticeships
Aspiration	Home ownership	Job security	Work-life balance	Freedom and flexibility	Security and stability
Attitude toward technology	Largely disengaged	Early information technology (IT) adaptors	Digital immigrants	Digital Natives	"Technoholics" – entirely dependent on IT, limited grasp of alternatives
Attitude toward career	Jobs are for life	Organisational — careers are defined by employers	Early "portfolio" careers — loyal to profession, not necessarily to employer	Digital entrepreneurs — work "with" organisations not "for"	Career multitaskers — will move seamlessly between organisations and "pop-up" businesses
Signature product	Automobile	Television	Personal Computer	Tablet/Smart Phone	Google glass, graphene, nano-computing, 3-D printing, driverless cars
Communication media	Formal letter	Telephone	E-mail and text message	Text or social media	Hand-held (or integrated into clothing) communication devices
Communication preference	Face-to-face	Face-to-face ideally, but telephone or e-mail if required	Text messaging or e-mail	Online and mobile (text messaging)	Facetime
Preference when making financial decisions	Face-to-face meetings	Face-to-face ideally, but increasingly will go online	Online — would prefer face-to-face if time permitting	Face-to-face	Solutions will be digitally crowd-sourced

*Percentages are approximate at the time of publication.

Figure 3.4: A guide to the generations currently living in the US.

Generational diversity in the classroom effects expectations, levels of experience, values and other aspects of the learning environment. The following illustration from the Generation Guide (2010) highlights some of the most pertinent comparisons.

Gens X, Y and Z

You will most frequently encounter Generations X, Y, and Z in your classroom. Generation X students were born between 1961 and 1980. They were "latch-key kids" of parents who were more likely than previous generations to be divorced. Gen Xers were raised to be independent and entrepreneurial, and though their generation gave birth to much of the technology we enjoy today, they probably didn't use it much in college themselves if they graduated before the mid-1990s (Novak, D., 2010). They are, therefore, "digital immigrants."

Millennials, also called Generation Y or the Echo Boomers, have comprised the largest cohort of students at the majority at colleges and universities until recently. Millennials have graduated or are graduating and moving into the workforce. Millennials, born between 1981 and 1995, are comfortable working in teams and have been nurtured by parents and educators throughout their academic lives. They have been told frequently by those around them that they are "special," and have high expectations for themselves (Novak, D., 2010).

The newest generation in our classrooms is Generation Z, or iGen, who were born between 1995 and 2010. These students are just starting to reach college age, but will soon be the majority of the "traditional" college students enrolled in colleges throughout the U.S. As with millennials, iGen college students have been raised on technology, and do not know a world without it. This makes both millennials and iGen "digital natives" with an inherent understanding of technology and an expectation of its use both inside and outside of the classroom. Generation Z students enjoy collaboration and active learning. Because they have grown up in the age of the search engine, they may not see the need for lecture and learning of basic information that may be found on their own. What they have not experienced, though, is the expectation that critical thinking may be required to determine the accurate from inaccurate information available to them (Novak, D., 2010).

Digital Natives vs. Digital Immigrants

Today's instructor will work with students with a variety of learning experiences. For instance, technology is one of the major differences between student generations, with some coming in as "digital natives" and others as "digital immigrants." Technology has changed our lives dramatically, so it should come as no surprise that it has brought about major changes in the field of education as well. Technology gives instructors broad and varied options with respect to how to teach, where to teach, and when to teach.

There will be some students who are perfectly comfortable using technology in the educational setting, and who may in fact even need technology in order to engage fully, and other students who are less comfortable with technology. Even among the students who are comfortable with technology, however, there are varied levels of experience with the types of technology used in education. For example, experience with social media does not prepare a student to participate in an online forum or teach the skills necessary to create a digital presentation.

Students With Disabilities

The modern student is more likely than any previous college student to acknowledge learning disabilities, experience issues related to mental health, and face other issues that may have previously been barriers to higher education. A study conducted by the National Alliance on Mental Illness (2012) states that:

"Colleges across the country are reporting large increases in the prevalence and severity of mental health conditions experienced by students attending their schools. This is good news for those living with these conditions since higher education is the foundation for securing stable employment and achieving financial independence. At the same time, it places pressure on schools to provide the services and supports that are necessary for these students to stay in school and to achieve academic success."

Approximately one fourth of Americans (26-28 percent) live with a diagnosable mental disorder. This includes a wide range of issues such as learning disabilities, attention difficulties, autism, depression, schizophrenia, and others (Kessler, Chui, Demler, Walters, 2005). According to Eisenberg, Golberstein, and Hunt (2009), mental health issues are associated with lower student achievement and higher drop-out rates. Some studies suggest that as many as 80 percent of college students have felt so overwhelmed by all they had to do in the previous year that they considered dropping out (American College Health Association).

Diagnoses of specific learning disabilities, including dyslexia, dysgraphia, and dyscalculia, as well as Attention Deficit Hyperactivity Disorder have increased by more than 30 percent in the last decade (American Academy of Pediatrics). Though 94 percent of high school students with learning difficulties receive assistance, only 17 percent of college students do. College has become more accessible, and supports are increasingly common, but instructors are likely to encounter students who are experiencing issues outside of the classroom that will affect their performance in the classroom. Students with such needs may have experienced intensive, individualized instruction prior to college, but are then expected to adjust to a lecture hall or classroom full of students moving at a pace different from their own.

Additionally, many students who are eligible to attend college are not academically prepared to do so. Depending on the admissions selectivity of your institution, you may find that less than half of your students are prepared for a college-level curriculum (Higher-education.org). This lack of readiness contributes to challenges in student retention and completion. The dichotomy between access and ability is one with which most colleges and college faculty must grapple. As a college instructor, you must devise and adopt strategies to successfully work with students of all ability levels so they are able to achieve the learning objectives of your course.

By now, we hope, you understand that your students will have different priorities, different backgrounds, different relationships with technology, and different educational goals. What does this mean for you as their teacher as you shape your course? Can you design a course in which all of these different students can learn the needed material and find success?

Using Student Demographics to Design Successful Courses

Can a lecture-based course meet all of the needs and challenges associated with educating the "modern student?" We hope you are beginning to understand why the answer to that question is no.

The ideal course (and instructor) for all of these students' needs must include at least these three aspects: training, support and flexibility.

First...Training

According to a report by the Association of American Colleges and Universities (2010), institutions should be prepared to offer training in new teaching pedagogies in order to reach the increasingly diverse student populations enrolled. Students must become engaged in the learning process, i.e. not just be passive recipients of information. Engaging the modern student requires instructors, courses and course materials which demonstrate openness, and teaching strategies which go well beyond the tried and true lecture.

Next...Support

Institutions may need to be prepared to offer training, but individual instructors need support, as well. As an instructor, you may feel isolated. You may not be introduced to the instructional technologist, the research librarian, or the distance learning specialist. You may not be invited to faculty meetings and professional development. So what do you do? Never fear! There are plenty of resources, discussion forums, and teachers excited to share what they do (like your friendly authors!) to help you along.

Last but not least...Flexibility

The ability to switch back and forth between different types of pedagogies is an important skill, and one that all faculty must develop. You may have students who learn best with visuals such as graphs and PowerPoints, while others learn best from hearing you talk about the material, and still others who may learn from reading a textbook. You may have students who take three hours to read the same pages another student finishes in less than an hour. You may even have students who cannot afford the textbook and enter the course hoping for the best!

Flipped and Blended Learning to the Rescue

As you will see in the coming chapters, flipped and blended learning is an excellent fit for a diverse, multi-generational classroom. You'll have the in-class time to provide the active, deep and individualized learning that the "modern student" needs. Now that your eyes are open to your audience, you are ready to learn more about what flipped and blended learning mean, and how exactly they can help you to engage your students and help them succeed.

> **Key Concepts:** *Pre-Planning Preparation*
> **Key Terminology:** *Tech Preparation, Lingo*
> **Key Idea:** *Prepare thoroughly before planning a flipped and blended course/lesson.*

CHAPTER 4
GETTING STARTED

The key to any successful course is preparation. A flipped and blended course is no different. We have talked about what to expect with flipped and blended learning, and why you might want to use it when planning your course. By now, perhaps you have decided that it is something that you may want to try, or at least explore further. Let's talk about the terminology you need to know and the skills you need to have in order to successfully flip and blend a course or lesson.

Lingo

Flipped and blended may be new terms to you, and they are not likely to be the only ones. Here are some common terms you'll encounter when reading or talking about flipped and blended learning:

Andragogy: Methods used to teach adult learners.

Asynchronous: A course structure or communication design in which the instructor and students are neither in the same room or online at the same time.

Blended Course: A course in which a portion of the coursework is completed online. The percentage of online versus face-to-face material may vary.

Chapter/Unit Learning Objective: Set by the book/instructor to meet course learning objectives (which are set by the state or institution). The instructor has some freedom to determine these objectives, as long as they are in line with the course objectives.

Course Learning Objective: Set by the state/institution and need to be met to ensure a standardized minimum of competency has been gained from this course.

Digital Immigrant: A student who has adapted to advances in technology, but was born before many current technologies (such as cell phones, tablets, etc.) were widely used. Usually applied to students who are part of Generation X or older age groups.

Digital Native: A student who has grown up with advanced technology. Usually applied to the Millenials and Gen Z.

E-Book: A book that has been published or translated into a format that allows for online viewing.

E-Learning: Learning that occurs in part or on whole online.

Face-to-Face: A term often used to describe classroom learning settings in which both the instructor and student are present in person. May be abbreviated "F2F."

Flipped Learning: A teaching model in which students experience the typical teaching and homework activities in reverse. Basic information provision is completed outside of the classroom, and active, deeper learning activities are completed within the classroom.

Formative Assessment: A range of formal or informal methods of assessing the effectiveness of learning activities in order to modify the activities or otherwise improve student learning. This type of assessment is most often low stakes, and the goal is to improve the effectiveness of teaching rather than to assess overall learning.

Hybrid Course: See "Blended Course."

Interactive Media: Resources or assignments that allow for two-way exchanges of information.

Learning Management System (LMS): A software platform that allows for delivery, tracking and assessment of online learning resources and assignments.

Online Learning: see "E-learning."

Pedagogy: Methods and practices of teaching of children. This term is also used as a global term to include the teaching of both children and adults.

Scaffolding: Creating course content that begins with a lot of support and structure for the learner and then tapers off as the learning gains knowledge and confidence.

Screen Capture: A type of electronic application that allows for the recording of a computer or device screen. This is often used for recording of lectures, webinars or other content delivery options for later viewing.

Summative Assessment: A form of assessment used to determine student learning at the end of an instructional unit. This type of assessment is usually medium to high stakes, and is used to evaluate results more than methods.

Tech Prep

Because flipped learning involves the delivery of basic information outside of the classroom, some basic technological knowledge is required. The knowledge you need depends on the resources you need to provide, the assignments you create, and the requirements of your college. Tech prep requires you to evaluate your hardware and software, and to prepare iron-clad back-up plans. You can count on technology both making your life easier and more difficult at times, so having a plan when things go wrong is an essential part of your tech prep.

What will you do if your wireless router breaks, or your internet service provider decides to do maintenance right in the middle of creating an online test? What would you expect your students to do? We expect our students to think ahead and have a plan, so having our own Plan B is an essential part of being an instructor in an online environment. In a blended and flipped course, you will face technological difficulties at some point. With adequate planning, you can avoid significant delays and interruptions.

Hardware

Computer: You need a personal computer as an instructor in a flipped and blended classroom. Whether that computer is a Mac or PC is up to you, either will allow you to do the necessary tasks.

 Check with your college regarding minimum software and hardware requirements. Some colleges offer faculty computer hardware and software purchasing discounts. Computer hardware and software manufacturers offer educator discounts, as well.

Camera and Microphone: If your computer does not already have a built-in webcam and/or microphone, it may be helpful to purchase an inexpensive one. This will help you to create content, communicate with your students, and access resources.

Data Backup: If you are not already in the habit of doing so, backing up your files at least weekly. An external storage device will help with privacy and organization of information, allowing you to store student files separately from your personal files.

 The basic external storage choices include USB flash drives, external hard drives and cloud storage. USB flash drives are portable and have varying storage capacity. However, they are easily misplaced and require a computer with a USB drive. An external hard drive is less portable, but is likely to have a higher storage capacity than a flash drive. Cloud storage is the most portable of all, requiring only the right applications and a good memory for passwords. Regardless of your choice of storage device, using one is an excellent idea.

Basic Protection Tools

Virus Protection: You will be downloading files created on your students' computers. Broad and reliable antivirus software is a necessity. If you are not familiar with this kind of software, consulting with the distance learning personnel at your college is a good idea, as is talking with the experts at an electronics or office store.

 Some of the most popular antivirus software makers are Norton, McAfee, and Kaspersky. You may also find that this type of subscription software is tax deductible. There are also excellent free antivirus software products for Mac and PC. Check *PC Magazine* for a list of the best free software available.

Adware and Spyware Protection: Adware and spyware can slow down your computer, or even bring it to a sudden halt, so scanning regularly is recommended. Your best bet is to choose an antivirus software that offers a full protection suite. There are a growing number of free tools out there, and many of them are browser extensions that integrate smoothly into your internet browser.

Basic Software

Word Processing: Your students will, most likely, submit their written work created with Microsoft Word. However, there are other popular document creation applications. Open Office is free and has the added benefit of being native to both Apple and PCs. Google Docs is cloud-based, free and accessible to anyone who registers for a free Google account.

Presentation: The most common presentation software is Power-Point by Microsoft. Google Slides is an easy-to-use free software, with the added benefit of allowing multiple users to work within the presentation at the same time, enabling easier group work.

Helpful Software and Applications

Screen Capture (Screen Shot): A screen capture is an image of a computer desktop that can be saved as a graphics file. Creating video content can be time-consuming, but there are a growing number of user friendly tools to make it easier. If you can create a slide presentation and have a built-in microphone on your computer, then you can create a video lecture. Several popular screen capture resources are made by TechSmith, including Snagit and Camtasia. There are free options as well, though, including Screencastify. With these and other applications, you can make and edit high quality video content for your students with very little technical knowledge.

Online Video Hosting: YouTube is the most popular video resource online, but it isn't the only one. Annenberg Media hosts its documentary series online, TedEd. Kahn Academy has an excellent lecture series. A benefit of YouTube and similar online video hosting sites, though, is that you can upload your own video content. Using a video host insures that you won't crowd your college's servers by uploading video directly into your course. With YouTube, you can post a link to a single video or an entire playlist, saving lots of time.

Video Conferencing: As a teacher of a flipped and blended course, you may wish to meet with your students online. For example, you may decide to hold virtual office hours, or you may want to provide a guest speaker outside of your regular classroom hours. Free applications such as Skype and Google Hangouts are usually sufficient for the needs of the flipped and blended instructor. There are more sophisticated (and more expensive) video conferencing resources out there, but they may not be as accessible to your students.

Course Design and Content Prep Strategies

Flipped learning requires organization and preparation of meaningful learning experiences. There is no room for last minute planning. Lessons must be prepared well in advance to allow students to prepare for each class. For instance, you will rarely lecture in class, but you still need to prep your lecturers so the information can be delivered in some form to your students outside of the classroom. You must also develop in-class active learning activities.

"The flipped classroom is an easy model to get wrong. Although the idea is straightforward, an effective flip requires careful preparation. Recording lectures requires effort and time on the part of faculty, and out-of-class and in-class elements must be carefully integrated for students to understand the model and be motivated to prepare for class" (Educause, Feb. 2012).

One of the most effective ways to prepare course content is to search for flipped learning modules created and shared by others. There are networks of teachers actively sharing materials and ideas. One such community is the Flipped Learning Network (www.flippedlearning.org). The website contains learning modules organized by subject. The group holds a yearly conference and sponsors an annual "Flip Day" to encourage teachers to give flipping a try.

In addition to using online sample materials when designing and prepping a flipped course, module or lesson, your teaching colleagues will be an excellent source of inspiration and ideas.

Finally, when designing your first flipped and blended course, start small. You may be excited and want to jump in and completely flip your entire course at once, but a better plan is to pick a single unit, module, or lesson to flip, and then add more lessons each time the course is taught. If you want to include a technology that is new to you, such as live chat, consider making it an option for the students instead of a requirement until you are completely comfortable and fluent with the technology.

Technology in education is a much debated subject today. Technological innovation in a society often exists simply because we want to make our lives better, our work more efficient, or our lives more satisfactory. Using technology can allow students and teachers to access resources, community and other educational tools.

By Ayra Sundbom

Flipped Instruction

Moving forward, we need to realize that college students have come to expect the integration of technology into their courses. Students react to technology generally in a positive light, which should encourage the instructor. That being said, using technology must add quantifiable value to your teaching. Sometimes a technological tool may be really interesting, but will not add value to your lesson or your course. In these instances, technologies should not be incorporated.

A technology which provides quantifiable benefits is the online gradebook in a Learning Management System (LMS). Students know that grades may be posted online. They expect this level of technology use from all of their instructors. Students assume (most often correctly) that if one instructor has access to a technology, all have access. Institutions differ in policies about using technology, so sometimes all instructors don't actually use a technological tool that is freely available to them. Demand from students can promote adoption of educational technologies in an institution and often inspires instructors to increase their technology use.

A major consideration concerning the use of tech in education, is the need to embrace change. Adopting new technologies is often time-consuming. Many times, the effort is heavily front-loaded. In essence, this requires an instructor to work double time to integrate a new technology into a course for a coming semester. This is why it is advisable for instructors to integrate changes gradually into their curriculum, rather than reinvent their courses all at once.

At the end of the day, tech is a human innovation. There will always be a "man behind the curtain," so to speak. Nonetheless, technology has changed the way that we (society) view (and practice) teaching and learning. Use of technology in higher education is about the relationships between teachers and students. Technology should add value to the course while achieving higher levels of understanding and a greater sense of satisfaction to the students and their instructor. — *Ayra Sundbom, MSID, Instructional Technologist, North Carolina Wesleyan University, North Carolina*

Key Concepts: *Planning*
Key Terminology: *Rigor vs. Busy Work, ADA Compliance*
Key Idea: *Planning ahead will allow the flipped and blended lesson to go smoothly, but flexibility is necessary.*

CHAPTER 5
CREATING THE FLIPPED FRAMEWORK

Let's review where we are in the process: We have discussed changing college student demographics and educational expectations, why a blended and flipped classroom works, how to get started and why leaving behind lecture-based instruction is crucial. Wow! That is a lot of information and we are not done yet. We have laid the groundwork to move into the next phase, the planning phase. Now it's time to tackle planning your first flipped lesson.

Begin With the End in Mind

Whether it's a full course or a single lesson, the best way to start when planning a learning activity or environment is with the desired outcome in mind. What will the learning look like? How will you know that the students have successfully mastered the course content? If you can answer questions such as these, you can successfully plan the steps necessary to reach your instructional goals.

Let's start with a single flipped lesson. What exactly will you need to plan? Here's a step-by-step guide:

1. **Learning Objective** – This is your goal. What will the learning look like when it has been achieved? What specific skills will the students have mastered or what information will they have learned?

2. **In vs. Out** – As discussed in previous chapters, you'll need to decide (using tools such as Bloom's Taxonomy) what

Flipped/Blended Lesson Planning Template

Lesson Topic:

Lesson Objectives:

Out-of-Class Activities:

Readiness Assessment:

Flipped Activities:

Assessment:

Resources/Items/
Preparation Needed:

Figure 5.1: Flipped and Blended Lesson Planning Template

activities happen inside of the classroom and which course materials can be covered effectively out of class.

3. **In Class** – What will you have the students do in the classroom? What are the resources needed? Will the students work in groups or individually? How many class sessions will the lesson require?

4. **Out of Class** – What knowledge do the students need in order to be prepared for the in-class work? What information is reasonable to cover using only video, lecture or homework activities? How will you assess the students' readiness/mastery?

5. **Assessment** – How will you assess whether the learning objective has been reached? What type of test, assignment or measurement can effectively show that the students have reached the learning objective?

Planning a full course using flipped and blended learning requires similar steps, only on a broader scale. You'll also need to take into account some of the traditional course planning requirements. Greive and Lesko in *A Handbook for Adjunct/Part-Time Faculty and Teachers of Adults* (2011) suggest the following steps as the ideal way to plan a course. These steps have been annotated with special considerations for the flipped classroom:

- **Course Outline Preparation** – Sell the course structure to the students. Remember that this is a standard course with no more or less work required than other course structures.

- **Textbook Choice** – With open educational resources and the availability of information online, a traditional textbook may not be necessary. Flipping a classroom allows for creative consideration of where the students will be getting course information.

- **Writing Behavioral Objectives** – Overall course objectives should be developed first, followed by individual module/ lesson objectives.

- **Laboratory Manual** (if a lab course)

- **Evaluation Methods** – Assess student readiness to begin the in-class work, and assess learning once the lessons are completed. Will there be an overall measure of learning at the end of the course? Is there a method of assessment more effective than a traditional test?

 Assignments – Both in-class and out-of-class work need to be designed and planned with instructional goals in mind. Active learning strategies are always best for a flipped classroom.

- **Developing Course Website** – A blended classroom is one where instruction is at least partly online. Your college's Learning Management System (Blackboard, Moodle, Canvas, etc.) will host your course for you. Your website needs to be organized to allow the students to navigate it easily.

- **Lecture Preparations** – Lectures won't take place in the flipped classroom in the same way as a traditional classroom. You will rarely talk for more than 5-15 minutes of a lesson. Lectures will be recorded and assigned to students to watch before class sessions.

- **Statement About Plagiarism**

- **Office Hours** – Placing any portion of a course online means offering virtual office hours. Evaluate your students' needs. Adjuncts may not be expected to hold scheduled office hours. However, having time during which students know they can reach you online (through Skype, chat, etc.) is important.

- **Placing Books on Reserve in Library**

- **Developing Pre-Tests (if required)** – Assessing student readiness before each class is a key feature of flipped learning. You must know that your students are ready, but a test is not necessarily the best or only way to do that.

- **Preparing Procedures on Test Re-Marking, etc.**

- **Developing the Assignment Attachments** – This is a somewhat time-consuming task in a flipped classroom. Much of the course material will need to be transitioned into the virtual environment. Make sure the students have what they need, and include links to resources such as tutoring centers, writing centers, helpful websites, etc.

The Importance of Learning Objectives

You can't know if your students have reached a goal (learning objective) if you don't know what behaviors should be observed when the students get there. This is why both of the course planning lists at the beginning of this chapter start off with learning objectives.

Learning objectives may be outlined for you by your institution, your department, or even the state or university system. As an instructor—particularly adjunct instructors—you will rarely be involved in the creation of goals at these levels, and it will be important to ask your supervisor what the learning objectives are before you begin to plan your course. The objectives are sometimes communicated as a list, but may also be presented as a course description or in another format.

In a blended and flipped class, the kinds of learning objectives that are under your control are the ones that you develop for each book chapter, course unit, module, lab or lesson. The question you want to answer is this one: What behaviors will show that the student has learned the material?

When planning chapter, course unit, module, lab or lesson objectives, begin by making sure that each of the chapter/topic objectives support the overall course learning objectives which your supervisor can provide. Sometimes the link between the two is direct and easily recognized, but at other times the link may be more indirect. Book chapter, course unit, module, lab or lesson objectives act as scaffolding (supports) to help the students reach the overarching course objectives. Your course objectives should increase in complexity as students move through the course materials and gain mastery.

Rigor vs. "Busy Work"

We hope by now you understand that flipping a classroom provides an exciting opportunity to take students much deeper into learning than can be done with lecture alone. However, in order to reach that goal, learning objectives and activities must be meaningful and deliberate. It is easy to develop activities, but much harder to make sure that all of those activities are meaningful, active learning experiences.

Avoid falling into the "busy work" trap. Review your chapter/topic objectives and verify that they all have a purpose directly related to the goals for the course. If they do not, set them aside or revise them so that they better align with the course learning objectives. The goal is to identify the most necessary components to the course and to straighten your path toward meeting the course learning objectives.

Transitioning an existing course to a blended and flipped one means more than simply digitizing your lectures and making PowerPoint slides. Evaluate your course materials and learning objectives, determine specific topics that need to be delivered by video/audio mini-lecture and which need to be covered in the classroom. Review chapter/topic objectives and strategize about technologies and tools that can help students learn. Your most important goal is to remove activities, assignments or course materials that do not work to meet the learning objectives for the class. Students must understand the purpose of each activity they do in the course and for each activity and assignment to be meaningful.

Don't Reinvent the Wheel

Why create twenty new lectures for your students if someone else has already done it? You may find an open resource course or set of lectures, a video series that explains core topics, interactive activities, articles, websites or podcasts that will not only help you cover the material, but will also help you to save significant preparation time. We will cover specific resources relevant to each part of the planning process as we move forward, but it's worth the time to point you in the right direction to begin exploring now.

YouTube

One of the first places to look for helpful resources is YouTube. Many of the documentaries that you watched when you were in school are now available on YouTube. You can also find lectures done by other instructors, student projects, television and movie clips. Organizations such as Annenberg Media and Study.com post initial sample lessons and videos on YouTube. TedEd has posted nearly all of its TedTalks on various channels and in various playlists. YouTube is also an easy way to share information, allowing you to create your own playlists which can then be shared using a single link with your students. For example, you can make a playlist for each chapter or module that you cover, for videos related to a single lesson, or for ancillary knowledge. There are other video hosting sites as well, such as Vimeo and Flickr.

Always be mindful of copyright, fair use and seek appropriate permissions when necessary. *Please see the Copyright & Fair Use Guidelines at the end of this book.*

The Internet

The internet has a wealth of websites created by faculty who teach your subject. You may find inspiration by viewing what others are doing, or resources that they have shared for general use. There are research projects online that may allow your students to act as subjects and take part in your chosen field experientially. There are also subject matter tutorials created by relevant organizations and placed online for general use. Any of these can be very helpful, and they may be of better quality than what you can produce yourself.

Textbook Publishers/Open Resources

Textbook publishers are another great source of course material, and they generally provide these resources without charge. Most publishers now also have an online component to their texts with interactive and adaptive exercises, e-book versions of textbooks, supplemental resources, and the ability to create quizzes and record lectures. These online components may be purchased by your students either in addition to or instead of a traditional printed text. Open educational resources are becoming more popular. These companies take the work out of curating resources. For example, OpenStax (www.openstax.org) has created introductory texts for a variety of subjects, and they have partnered with a number of companies to both curate and create content for students for a modest fee.

Peers

The final and possibly best resource to help you avoid reinventing the wheel is your peers. Online networks of professionals such as the Flipped Learning Network (www.flippedlearning.org), Facebook groups and pages, listservs, email lists and professional organizations can be invaluable sources of information. On campus professional development and departmental meetings can help you network with your peers, while professional conferences are endless sources of ideas. Contacting your college's librarians and instructional leaders or coaches can produce a wealth of ideas and materials. Connect with your peers in some way, and you'll find an endless source of inspiration for flipped lessons and inject excitement in your teaching.

Challenges Faced by Flipped Learning Facilitators

Challenges come in many shapes and sizes, but there are a few consistent hurdles faced by flipped learning facilitators.

- **Student Buy-In:** Some students will actively and rapidly embrace a change from the traditional lecture. Others will long for the familiar "sage on the stage." Some students like lectures because they can forego preparing for class and count on you to feed them what they need for "the test." Getting students excited about a flipped classroom is not only in the initial selling of the idea, but also the consistent follow-up on your initial promises.

- **Stakeholder Buy-In:** One issue that we faced when blending and flipping our courses was that our supervisors did not understand the pedagogy. There is a pervasive misunderstanding of the flipped classroom. It was difficult at times to make sure that the classes were seen as equivalent, and that stakeholders understood and respected varied pedagogy. The best tools to convince stakeholders to buy in are student retention and engagement data which will improve with a flipped classroom and active learning.

- **Accountability:** In order to be successful, students have to complete the outside work before arriving for class. However, students in lecture classes are often not used to being held accountable for preparation, so it presents a challenge for them. Plan assignments or minute papers to test students' basic knowledge before moving forward.

- **Student Readiness:** Some of the students who enter your classroom will not be prepared with the basic reading, writing and study skills needed to be successful in college. Be prepared with links to helpful resources, contacts at tutoring and counseling centers on your campus and information from sources such as your campus librarians. Your department chair can be a helpful contact to obtain information about remediation resources on campus and support services for students who are underprepared.

- **Infrastructure Challenges:** Classrooms at many colleges are not set up to facilitate group activities and active learning. In addition, the larger your class, the more likely you are to be assigned to a lecture hall whose seating makes working in groups challenging. Internet access may be unreliable at times, and classrooms may or may not be set up to accommodate the use of multimedia. There are ways to work around all of these issues with planning, but it's a good idea to evaluate the classroom you're going to be using as early as possible so you can make adjustments as needed.

- **ADA and Accessibility:** Accessibility for all students is key when planning the course that you will teach, whether it's a traditional lecture or an active learning activity. ADA compliance means providing transcripts, closed captioning, or other accommodations. When you make your own video resources, be sure to use a script so you can provide it as a transcript, and be sure to use formatting that allows for ADA compliance. It is also a good idea to provide information in several different formats, such as video, audio, written, interactive, etc.

- **Developing a Large "Toolbox":** Flexibility is one of the key factors to being a successful flipped learning facilitator. You are likely to have to switch gears at least once during the semester due to technological issues such as a malfunctioning video. You may also have students complete a readiness assessment and learn that they have struggled with an entirely different concept than you were planning to cover during the class period that day. Guest speakers cancel on you. Having a big "tool box" will allow you to have multiple resources planned and ready to go if something like this happens. Over time, you will gradually build a large collection of activities to cover each topic in your course. It's not necessary to have this collection complete for your first flipped lesson or course, but always be ready to do a mini-lecture on a topic.

- **Availability of Equipment:** College students come from many different socioeconomic backgrounds, and may have varied access to technology. Some of your students may have easy access to cell phones, tablets and computers, but some may have to visit a public or campus library to access the internet. Keep this in mind when planning out-of-class work. As instructors at a community college with a very diverse student body, one way that we handle this is to do an informal survey at the start of a course to see what technological strengths and needs exist. Your situation may vary, but some ways that we handle this are to design classroom teams that have at least one member who can bring a portable device like a tablet or laptop to class, make outside work available as early as possible so students can access it when it is convenient to them, and to have our courses designated as "hybrid" so there is an understanding of the need for technology access from the start.

Be understanding, set reasonable limits, and get to know what resources are available for free or low cost to your students through your institution and public libraries. There is almost always a free option, and it's worth taking the time to find it for students who need it.

As we have stressed previously, start small, plan ahead, have a backup, and be ready to go with the flow. A little flexibility will go a long way toward ensuring the positive outcomes associated with the use of flipped and blended learning.

Now that you are ready to plan your course, it's time to take a look at the elements involved in a flipped lesson. Before you move forward, prepare a table of contents for your course or a list of course learning objectives. You'll be able to use it as a handy reference as we move into the mechanics of course creation. As you plan, highlight the topics you feel you can flip most easily and start with those.

It's ultimately more productive to have a few quality flipped lessons than to have an entire course partially completed, so take this at your own pace. If you feel that you're ready to dive in and flip everything, then by all means go for it! However, don't be afraid to flip a single lesson at first and then move forward from there.

CHAPTER 6
FLIPPING YOUR CLASS (OUT-OF-CLASS WORK)

By now you know that planning is critical to this process and if you have prepared your list of course learning objectives (see Chapter 5), you are well underway. If you haven't, no worries. However, remember that you will make changes to your course plan after you've used it the first time, and you need to have a firm foundation on which to build your blended and flipped course.

Let's move into the nitty-gritty of flipping. This chapter will show you how to prepare and deliver the out-of-class work that students in your flipped course will need to complete prior to attending class. This is an important piece of the blended and flipped classroom, since the success of your in-class activities hinges on the knowledge students gain outside of the classroom.

Ideas and How-To

Any of these ideas can be turned into an assignment or a "ticket to enter" (more about this later). There are multiple strategies to help a student learn the basic information s/he needs to learn outside of class in a flipped classroom. Plan to explore and use more than one activity or format. Here are some ideas to get you started.

- **Readings (Textbook, Online, Articles):** Whether it is a printed textbook or an e-book, reading is critical. However, many students do not know how to read the textbook effectively, and might have trouble completing out-of-class assignments. Provide additional structure, especially early on in the semester to help students improve reading comprehension skills. Have students outline the chapters. Provide them with guided notes and/or questions, reflective questions, or reading guides. Students will learn to prioritize the important information from their reading instead of being overwhelmed by it.

- **Online Videos:** Sites such as YouTube, Khan Academy, and Udemy offer many open access videos. These videos can augment your own videos or be used in place of video materials you might create. In addition, there are many free software options that allow you to edit these videos and insert questions. (Please refer to the Copyright & Fair Use Guidelines in this book.)

- **Interactive Websites:** The availability of online tutorials (https://www.gcflearnfree.org/fractions/), interactive exercises and other such resources may be limited for some disciplines. However, there are many open source interactive websites that allow a student to experience the topic you are teaching. For example, introductory psychology students can use an interactive website to train Pavlov's dog (https://www.brainpop.com/games/pavlovsdog/). Biology students can travel through the brain (http://www.innerbody.com/image/nervov.html). Students can then write a reflection of their experiences or explain their experience.

- **Webquests and Internet Scavenger Hunts:** Activities in this category include guided searches for information (https://sites.google.com/site/csiscavengerhunt101/), and the subsequent reporting of that information and possibly reflection on the experience. The results can be shared in class, or can be submitted through the LMS. Students can complete discussion boards, video assignments, blogs, presentations or journal entries. The goals should be individualized, allowing for the student to be creative, reflective and think critically.

- **Publisher Content:** Textbook publishers create content that can be used in conjunction with their textbooks. This content is perfect for flipped learning. Resources include flashcards, crossword puzzles or videos with questions. Assigning these as out-of-class work will help students structure their out-of-class time.

- **Framing the Information:** Create a template of sentences that helps students locate important information in the outside assignment. Framing the information is similar to guided notes, but allows students to think critically and make connections within the material. This is a great resource to use early in the semester.

- **Online Lectures/Screencasts:** Recording your own online lectures is the easiest way to make sure that students are getting the information they need. If you teach a traditional lecture section of the course you want to flip, record yourself now, before you change formats. You can edit those lectures into smaller mini-lectures to share with your students. Typically, screencasting involves presentation slides and a voice-over, although some instructors make their faces visible during the recording. There are several free and low-cost screencast programs. For example, Screencastify is a Google add-on that not only works with the programs that are part of Google Drive, but can save your video to Google Drive for easy sharing. Your college's Distance Learning Department may be able to provide you with excellent screencasting resources, and the training needed to use them.

Online Lecture and Screencasting Tips

When making online lectures, you will need a written transcript so you can complete or correct the closed captioning needed to make your course content accessible to all of your students. When creating online lectures and screencasts, keep your lectures under five minutes. It is better to have three five-minute lectures posted in you LMS than one 15-minute lecture. The four numbered tips on the following two pages are important to remember and implement (Winstead, 2016):

1. Engaging Text is Half the Battle

Someone might argue that text is just a necessary evil in a video lecture, and you should be paying more attention to visuals and the tone of your voice. There is some truth in this, yet your message should always be reinforced with readable text. Keep it short and simple (K.I.S.S.), after all, it's just a brief lesson, not a doctoral thesis. As with voice recording and animations, presentational writing has its dos and don'ts.

Starting with the don'ts – never use all caps or mixed fonts unless proving a point or drawing on a highly specific context. Inconsistent fonts look unprofessional and imply the author's negligence – an effect you definitely want to avoid. Also, stay away from the Times New Roman font – almost any option is better: Sans Serif, Arial, Calibri, or preferably a custom font if you have the resources.

2. Creatives and Colors: A Picture is Worth a Thousand Words

Seeing the teacher live is a blessing, but you always need to substantiate your point and make it more accessible to the viewers. In this regard, visuals are hard to overestimate. Screencasting software like Camtasia enables the instructor to share the screen with the audience and display many types of content right from the computer.

In any case, don't let the text eclipse the look and feel of your course. Use pertinent images to illustrate your key points. Avoid standard PowerPoint imagery and go the extra mile to add tailored visuals. Once you have an image on a slide, try to review its contents and decide whether the text is indispensable, or if you can do without it. If you can, let the picture speak for itself.

3. Audio Tips: What You Hear is What You Get

When recording narrations, make sure you create a good working environment to minimize possible distractions. Keep your location quiet. If you are recording a live class at the whiteboard, repeat students' questions to keep up the integrity of your discourse, and avoid off-record comments or private chats.

In a classic setup where it's just you and your webcam, consider stand-alone equipment instead of an embedded microphone. Don't forget to do a short test run before you've made too much progress. Once you are finished, eliminate bloopers, redundancies and pauses. Make sure your course dynamics are unimpaired.

4. Get Feedback Right Away, or Allow Summary Questions

You might want to take your lecture to the next level and turn it into a dialogue. Don't hesitate to put your discourse on hold and check to see if the audience catches your drift. Use special software like Zaption to embed interactive questionnaires that your students have to fill in as they watch. This way you will understand whether your lectures are on the right track, and you can adjust your course to cover difficult issues.

Built in quizzes boost engagement and self-assessment. Let them remain ungraded. The key point is to get quick feedback and see what you can improve. Bridge the gleaned information with a learning management system (LMS) for better analysis and follow up.

Technological Resource Round-up

What follows is a list of some of our favorite resources to use in our blended and flipped classrooms:

- **YouTube:** Videos on almost any topic you can imagine. If you cannot find quality videos here to supplement the teaching, start thinking outside of the box. For example, a nursing instructor was looking for a video on the steps needed to maintain a sterile area, but could not find a good one. She then found a mediocre one, had the students watch it and list all of the mistakes that were made on the video.

- **Khan Academy:** Videos on a variety of subjects. Allows you to do a keyword search to locate videos that cover the information. These videos are generally short and give the information in a streamlined way.

- **TedEd:** This site contains a variety of short talks (about 20 minutes long) by dynamic speakers. They can be used to help students see another viewpoint of a topic, to encourage them to think critically, or just to learn something new.

- **Zaption - Interact With Video:** Create a Zaption tour from your own video library, or from clips on YouTube.

- **AP Websites:** There are many websites aimed at AP classes. If you teach an introductory course, you might be able to find content, ideas and worksheets that are useful.

- **Screencast-O-Matic:** Free screen and webcam recorder to record on-screen activity for short tutorials and visual presentations. Publish to YouTube or save as a video file.

- **Remind:** (www.remind.com) This is a free text reminder service students can use. It protects the privacy of the instructor's cell phone number, but allows you to text your entire class or one student. You can set up reminders to go out at specific times. We find this service useful to remind students to complete their outside assignments or to bring items, such as laptops, to class.

Holding Students Accountable

You may be wondering whether you will get students to complete the out-of-class work. The honest answer is that you may never get 100 percent compliance. There will be times when the students are unsure of the assignment, so they either do not complete the out-of-class work, or they do the wrong assignment. Sometimes life happens and even your best students might not complete the out-of-class coursework. However, in our experience, we have found that well-planned, well-executed outside assignments result in much higher rates of completion and deeper levels of understanding.

Roadblocks

A few years ago, at a campus function to which community members had been invited, we spoke to a librarian from the local public library. We learned that many of our students used the library's resources for school work. These students often had questions about our LMS and how to complete different tasks in it, and the librarians were often unable to help the students. After consulting with our school administration, we offered a short training to be held at their library on our LMS software. The librarians were excited to have this opportunity and our students had an additional source of support.

So, what can you do to address the challenge of unprepared students? Here are some recommendations:

1. Have a conversation with any student who is not prepared for class to determine why that student did not come to class with the out-of-class assignment completed.

This should be a private, non-threatening conversation. Think of it as a fact-finding mission. As long as the student could have completed the assignment and chose not to, the next step is to explain why it is important to do so in the future, connect the consequence for non-completion, and stress your faith that the student will be able to move ahead in the class as long as the out-of-class work is completed. This usually is a good way to jump-start a student's participation.

2. Review your pre-class assignment.

"The flipped classroom is a partnership....You plan the activities. They engage in the activities. You teach by guiding from the side. They learn by doing. One of your responsibilities is to design the pre-class assignment. Is it clear what the students are supposed to do? Is it too demanding? Does it take too much time? Is it confusing? Could it be organized more effectively? Sometimes a simple adjustment in the pre-class assignment is all you need to do to improve student preparedness" (Honeycutt, 2016).

3. Make sure students have access to necessary resources

During the conversation, you may find out the students lack critical resources to complete the assignment. A few times each semester, we discover students in our blended and flipped classes who don't have a computer and/or internet access. Steer the conversation to available resources that the student can access such as campus libraries, city libraries, computer labs and learning centers.

 If the student has a smartphone, there are many places the student can go to access free Wi-Fi, such as local coffee shops and restaurants. If your LMS is not mobile compliant, be sure to let the students know its limitations. For example, our LMS will allow students on a mobile device to submit work and look at content, but may or may not register a test score if the student takes a test on it. So we urge our students to take tests at a library using a computer there.

4. Re-think participation grades.

If you build in participation grades as part of your grading policy, then make "completing pre-class work" a significant part of the participation and final grade.

"This approach also permits students to have more control over their choice in whether to come prepared. They know the consequences in terms of how their lack of preparation affects their grade" (Honeycutt, 2016).

5. Make sure that to successfully participate in the in-class activity, the outside work must have been completed.

The student will learn that s/he is not prepared to participate in class, and may even earn some low grades because of a lack of preparation.

If you have multiple students who did not complete the work, or if the work is done incorrectly, then it is time to look at your assignment and the instructions you gave. More likely than not, there was a problem with one of those. It is also a good idea to talk with the students to ask them what their thought processes were. Once you have isolated the problem with the assignment, fix it before using the assignment with other students.

Life Happens

What happens when a strong student, or a student who is usually prepared comes to class without having completed the outside assignment?

Generally, a conversation with the student is in order. Many times, it is a situational issue that has resolved itself, such as a sick child or having to work overtime. In this case, having the conversations helps the student to know you care, and helps to motivate the student to be prepared for class in the future. It is important to remember that life happens to people. Build in some room for a student to complete work late or miss an assignment. This way your conversation with the student who misses an assignment is one of support and hope.

 To make certain your students complete out-of-class work, plan it carefully, make your expectations clear and provide consequences for incomplete work.

We are invariably asked about the amount of grading required. As with so many aspects of blended and flipped learning, you have a variety of options. One option is to randomly grade assignments. That is to pick a certain number of assignments through the semester to grade. The students do not know which assignments will be graded, so they complete them all. Another idea is to grade on completion. Assignments that are turned in complete are graded as completed. You can also marry both of these and randomly grade some for content and the rest for completion.

How to Make Sure Flipped Coursework Gets Completed

Remember that with the flipped coursework, we are focusing on the lower levels of learning in Bloom's Taxonomy. Therefore, we want to help the students to begin memorizing and understanding class content.

Complete the planning of the lesson using the information from the previous chapter. Decide on how to attain your learning objectives, which work is to be done out of class (the flipped work) and which work will be accomplished in the classroom. Remove the busy work and made sure that the assignment is appropriately rigorous for your class.

Clearly-Presented Flipped Assignments

While it sounds obvious, the very first step is to share the flipped assignment with the students. Your students must understand how to complete the assignment, what is expected from them on this assignment and how this assignment is going to be connected to future learning in the class. This means that it is important to give the students a clear vision of what must be done. This could include detailed instructions, learning objectives for the activity, an example of a successful attempt of the activity, or a grading rubric which outlines expectations.

After introducing the outside activity, it is important to explain the consequence of not completing the required work. These consequences can range from excluding the student from the class activity while they complete the missing work, to a zero in participation points, or even a zero on the class activity. Students are busy people, so understanding the consequence can help them to be motivated to complete the assignment.

Let's run through some examples of outside activities how to introduce them and ideas for making sure they are completed (the consequences).

Tickets to Enter

The first two ideas we want to present are "Ticket to Enter" and quizzes. The ticket to enter (below) is just that. A student must complete some task and bring to class evidence of completion. These tickets to enter can be worksheets, summaries, items found on the internet, or anything that they can present that proves that they have completed the work. If the ticket to enter is a document, it may help to have the students submit it to your LMS prior to the beginning of class to limit students copying other's work. This ticket to enter can then be used as a grade for the class.

Theory A is useful in that it states _____ which helps to support the ideas of _____. However, theory A has some significant weaknesses, which include _____. Theory B is useful in that it states _____ which helps to support the ideas of _____. However, theory A has some significant weaknesses, which include _____. Three main differences between Theory A and Theory B are _____.

Figure 6.1: Ticket to Enter

Quizzes

Quizzes may be used multiple ways. You can give individual quizzes, or if you use small groups, you can give group quizzes. You could even give the quiz to individuals, then again to the group and average the grades. Allowing the group to discuss the questions can lead to engagement and learning.

When using quizzes to measure completion of out of class work, you can use multiple choice tests, which are quick to grade, peer grading where they exchange quizzes, or an online LMS quiz which can automatically grade the quiz.

Once you have created your out-of-class assignment, decide how you are going to make sure you have compliance from your students. Are you going to collect the work as a ticket to enter? Will it be submitted online or in person at the beginning of class? Will the students need to complete a quiz? Will it be done before class or in class? If you give the quiz in class, will they complete it individually or in groups? How much of the student's grade will depend on this work?

Connect the Work

Finally, you need to make sure that you connect the out-of-class work to the in-class work, and all of the student work to your learning objectives. A well thought out flow between in-class work and out-of-class work is important to help the students connect the importance of each type of work in your flipped and blended class.

 Now it's time to begin planning the in-class, active learning portion of your flipped and blended class. Remember that with the in-class work, we are focusing on the higher levels of learning in Bloom's Taxonomy. Therefore, we want to help the students to begin analyzing class content thereby leading to deeper understanding.

You will be limited only by your imagination when you start planning and integrating active learning strategies into your lessons.

> **Key Concepts:** *Active Learning*
> **Key Terminology:** *Active Learning, Collaborative Learning, Busy Work*
> **Key Idea:** *Preparation enables active learning thus allowing deeper examination of course material.*

CHAPTER 7
FLIPPING YOUR CLASS (IN-CLASS WORK)

Your students are prepared with the basic knowledge needed for their face-to-face (in-class) instruction/learning sessions. They have watched the lectures, completed activities and tutorials, and shown you through readiness assessments that they are prepared for the next steps. Since your class time won't be spent giving a long lecture to deliver basic information, what will you do when you are face-to-face with your students in a blended and flipped class?

This is where the process can feel somewhat daunting for instructors who are wedded to the lecture model. Figuring out what to do with your students that isn't "busy work" is not only important, but it's the key element that makes your learning environment flipped *and* blended. You get to be creative now, and maybe even have time to do all of those fantastic demonstrations and projects that you never managed to work in to your lecture courses, or sent home with the students as out-of-class homework. Instead of fumbling through these kinds of assignments on their own, they now get to have the benefit of your knowledge and experience as they work through them. As an added bonus, you get to watch it all click into place!

In-class activities in a flipped and blended classroom are learning elements which engage students in the material, create opportunities for collaboration, foster critical thinking and analysis, and allow application. The flipped and blended classroom activities are opportunities for students and faculty to be creative in a low-stakes environment.

The activities that you choose to use in the classroom should be linked to your course objectives very clearly. It is helpful to show the students how they connect, or have them show you. For example, you can include your objectives on a set of written instructions, take a few moments to talk about the links, or even design your entire course around your objectives in a visible and purposeful way. No matter how you do it, it is important for the students to understand that this isn't just a time to do busy work or leave them feeling as though they are teaching themselves.

 In our opinions, the best part of a flipped and blended classroom environment is that it provides opportunities for creativity and fun. We can add global content to allow students to explore concepts from different cultural perspectives. We can share with them our own excitement about our fields and how to apply the concepts they're learning. We not only foster teamwork, but also give them valuable experience practicing the "soft skills" that employers are seeking.

The key to a successful flipped and blended classroom is active learning. Active learning can take many forms, and your discipline will determine much of what you do in the classroom, but there are some common active learning elements. In their presentation "Strategies to Incorporate Active Learning into Online Teaching," Diane Austin and Nadine Mescia (2001) suggest that strategies for active learning are the same whether employed in traditional lecture, online, or alternative course designs such as flipped and blended learning. According to Austin and Mescia, active learning should:

1. Have a definite beginning and ending;
2. Have a clear purpose or objective;
3. Contain complete and understandable directions;
4. Have a feedback mechanism;
5. Include a description of the technology or tool being used in the exercise.

When planning an active learning activity, here are some things to consider, courtesy of the University of Minnesota Center for Educational Innovation:

- What are your objectives for the activity?

- Who will be interacting? Will students pair up with someone beside them or someone sitting behind/in front of them? Should they pair up with someone with a different background? Someone they don't know yet?

- When does the activity occur during the class? Beginning? Middle? End? How much time are you willing to spend on it?

- Will students write down their answers/ideas/questions or just discuss them?

- Will students turn in the responses or not? If they are asked to turn them in, should they put their names on them?

- Will you give individuals a minute or so to reflect on the answer before discussing it or will they just jump right into a discussion?

- Will you grade their responses or not?

- How will students share the paired work with the whole class? Will you call on individuals randomly or will you solicit volunteers?

- If students are responding to a question you pose, how are you going to ensure that they leave with confidence in their understanding? (Often, if various student answers are discussed without the instructor explicitly indicating which ones are "right," students become frustrated. Even with a question that has no absolute "right" answer, students want to know what the instructor's stand on the question is.)

- What preparation do you need to use the activity? What preparation do the students need in order to participate fully?

In-class activities can be individual, paired, informal small group, or more complex cooperative activities. Your choice of activity will depend largely on your discipline, but also on the class size, the type and size of space available (lab, computer lab, classroom with tables, lecture hall, etc.), the time you have to devote to the activity, and your comfort level with the course material and tools.

Challenges to Successful Active Learning

The biggest challenge to a successful active flipped and blended learning classroom activity is preparation. If you have planned correctly to hold students responsible for the out-of-class work, then this challenge is easily overcome. You are likely to have some unprepared students at first as they get used to the new course structure, but be consistent with your readiness assessment and you will overcome that challenge.

Another challenge may be your students' aversion to "group work." We frequently face this roadblock with students who have had bad experiences with group projects in high school and in other college courses. Not all active learning activities are cooperative, but a flipped and blended classroom does offer a wonderful opportunity to help students sharpen these skills. We find that the best way to overcome this challenge is to allow students time to build rapport within their teams. For example, in larger projects, we have both successfully used the strategy of having students assign themselves roles and jobs that are uniquely theirs within the group. Developing a creative team name has also proven effective in building unity among team members.

"Active and collaborative learning necessarily results in a great deal of student talk, leading to noisy classrooms. Combine that with the potential visual cues from multiple screens installed on the walls of active learning classrooms, and you have an environment that can be overwhelming to some students and easily lead to distractions and off-task behavior in others" (University of Minnesota Center for Educational Innovation). A flipped and blended classroom is loud! Getting used to that can take some time, but it's definitely worth it.

Do you remember those pet peeves we discussed in the first chapter? Due to the nature of active learning, cell phone usage in the classroom, side conversations and sleeping during class happen much less frequently. If they do, be creative. If you see a student texting instead of participating in teamwork, ask him or her to research a topic related to one of your courses objectives using the internet. Create a "tech break" during which everyone in class races to find a fact about the day's topic.

Finally, in order to employ active learning effectively, your own knowledge of the subject matter has to be deep. Once students are given the opportunity to think critically and analytically about the course material, you will get questions beyond what will be on the test. Can you be ready for that? Of course you can! This is the subject you spent years learning and perfecting after all.

Tips for Active Learning Activities

Here we go with what you've been waiting for! The following list is not in any way exhaustive, nor is it discipline specific. These ideas and strategies will get you started on your way to an active, flipped and blended classroom.

Concept Maps

This assignment asks students to visually map concepts, finding connections between them and opening an opportunity for further discussion. Students can work individually, collaboratively, or in a combination of the two options.

Polling

Electronic clickers and apps can be used, or this can be as simple as raising hands or using chalk/white boards. This is a good way to quickly survey understanding, expose the wide variety of possible opinions/responses, and spark discussion.

Minute Papers

Minute papers can be used at any point in the class session, including use as an exit activity. There are many possibilities for variation, and this can also be used as a formative assessment. One useful variation is to ask students to add their own question at the end to increase reflection. That question can then be answered personally, or used in a group activity in which students exchange papers and answer another student's question. Doing this type of activity before a classroom discussion also has the benefit of allowing more introverted students to gather their thoughts and feel better prepared for discussion.

Think/Pair/Share

This activity employs both individual and collaborative work. Students initially work individually, thinking through their ideas and writing them down as needed. Next, students pair and discuss their ideas with their partners. Finally, ideas are shared with the class as a whole. This can be a useful preparation for another activity, such as polling or debate, or can stand alone.

Round Robin

There are several phases to this activity, and it can be a good way to get students up and moving around the classroom. Small groups begin by brainstorming about a question or concept, creating a written record of their thoughts. This initial phase requires the most time. The groups then leave their written record behind and migrate to another group's station. They review what the previous group wrote about their topic/question, and are given a short time to delete, correct, and add to the list. Once time is up, the groups migrate again and repeat the delete/correct/add process. The activity ends when all groups have responded to all written records. This can be a useful preparation for classroom discussion, polling, or debate, or can stand alone.

Game/Quiz — Creating and Repurposing

Many pre-made games and game applications exist and are useful in the classroom. For example, having students develop their own teaching games can be both fun and educational. Board and traditional games such as Monopoly, Life, Sorry, bingo, Jeopardy, Family Feud and others can be used to teach concepts in many courses. Students can also use the boards and create their own rules and accessories to develop their variations. For example, Monopoly can be used to teach stratification. Simply by stratifying the money and property according to U.S. Census data, microcosms of society are created. It helps students to better understand the disparity of wealth and poverty in USA in a way that can never be achieved in a lecture.

Role Play

Students assume roles and act out parts to illustrate concepts, theories, or perspectives on a topic. Traditionally used for in-class activities, this can be adapted for online courses using video resources and discussion boards. An essential element of this assignment, though, is a reflective discussion.

Fishbowl

A small group of students engage in a mediated discussion of a topic. The remaining students arrange themselves around the smaller group, and observe while taking notes with critiques and questions. Once the inner circle is finished, the outer circle discusses the interactions and provide additional insight into the topic.

Sorting

Though this can be as simple as having students raise hands, it is a good way to get them up and moving in the classroom. A series of sorting criteria are needed. Students self-select their sorting groups by moving to stand with others in a designated spot once the first set of criteria is announced. They move again with the next set of criteria, and again with the next. This can continue as long as needed, and can include discussion along the way. It is a good, active alternative to polling, and can be an effective icebreaker.

Debate

This activity can include out-of-class preparation or be completed entirely in the classroom. Individuals or teams of students take opposing viewpoints and present general information. They are then given time to respond to the other viewpoint, taking turns to continue the debate until time is up or the goal of the debate has been reached. Reflection by the rest of the class is a good addition to an assignment like this.

Create a Quiz

Quiz apps exist to make this just as effective for an online class as a seated class. Students can create any type of question desired by the instructor. For example, they may create essay questions, or they may be asked to create multiple choice questions that can be inserted into a clicker or polling application.

Case Studies

Case studies allow for deep exploration of a single individual or group, or a single theory or concept. The format is flexible, and can be used in many classes. It allows for application of concepts to real-life scenarios, and can help students to understand how theoretical concepts fit the world around them.

Jigsaw

In a jigsaw activity, students are initially divided into groups and given a topic to research. They become "experts" on their topic and develop lesson plans to share their knowledge with their classmates. The experts from each topic group are then dispersed into new groups that contain one expert from each topic. Each expert takes a turn to teach the group to which they have moved, allowing all students to learn about all of the topics by the end of the activity.

Best Example Contest

Learning terminology can be moved to a new level by asking students to provide examples instead of definitions. Creating original examples requires an understanding of the definition beyond memorization. Students can share their examples in a contest format, giving them a chance to reflect on and correct their own understanding as they are exposed to other examples. They vote on or rate the examples presented, and a winner is declared by popular vote. There are many format options for this type of activity, so it is adaptable to many classroom settings and situations.

Cell Phones

Almost all of the students in the class carry a smart phone. You can create instant application by giving teams of students a list of terminology and set them loose on campus to capture something that they believe represents their words. Have student upload pictures to your LMS and pull them up as the students explain why they felt it represented their word.

Cell phones can also be used to create short infomercials about a topic in your class. Smart phones have editing software built in that will create a short video on the topic you select. Once the videos are created, share them with the class and talk about the information given. These can also be posted on LMS or on Youtube (which will allow for closed captioning).

Know and Need to Know

This allows students to identify their levels of knowledge and to understand areas that they might need to increase their knowledge. Have students divide a piece of paper in half. On one side, list everything they know about the prompt given. On the other side of the paper, have them identify things they still need to learn. Put the students into teams of 4-6 to compare their lists.

Speed Dating Study Session

Have each student prepare a question or information pertaining to the topics that are being covered. Set the students up in two rows facing each other. Give them two minutes to share their information and then call time. One row of students move to the next person and the time starts over. This is a great way to have students review a lot of material in a short amount of time.

Build a Model

This technique uses manipulatives to build a model or solve a problem. For example, in a psychology or biology class, students may be asked to use clay to build a brain. Or in a business class a student may be asked to build a prototype of a product to sell. In a chemistry class students may be asked to build models of molecules. The options are endless.

Technology Tools

Technology doesn't have to be limited to outside of the classroom. Most students will at least have a smart phone in class, and many will have a laptop or tablet. Some of the tech tools that we have found useful in the classroom include:

Remind (www.remind.com)

Remind is a text reminder service to which your students can subscribe. It keeps your cell phone number private, but allows you to text students, individually or as a group. If you would like to, you can allow students to text you back. Remind can be used for reminding students of due dates; but it is much more helpful than that. You can remind students to bring items to class. If you are running late or have a last minute room change, you can notify students in real time. If you get the app for your phone, you can contact students from your phone.

Google Drive

The Google Drive suite of resources is available for free to everyone with a Gmail-based email address. Not only does it provide free access to word processing, spreadsheet and presentation software, but it also allows for real-time collaboration. Students can collaborate on or off campus, teachers can collaborate over lesson plans, students across the world can work on the same document, videos and webspace can be created, and much more.

Plickers

Allows you to poll your class. Each student gets their own individual Plicker card. Simply by scanning the classroom with your device, you can take roll or get answers to questions (yes, no, A, B, C, or D). Different answers register by the way that students hold their card. You get real time information about individuals and their knowledge base.

Screencast Software

You can get Google Screencastify or PowerPoint Office Mix for free. This allows you a lot of creativity in developing lectures to post online, but it can also be used in the classroom to help students create presentations or record their own demonstrations. These tools enable students to collaborate with students in other courses on a joint project. (Author Note: In a psychology course, the students recorded presentations about various mental health diagnoses and mental health stigma and sent them to students in a graphic design course. The graphic design students then created anti-stigma posters based on what they learned and submitted them to a large-scale mental health awareness event that both classes attended.)

Kahoot (www.getkahoot.com)

Create a fun learning game online. Send students the PIN number to your game and invite them to play. Students download the app to their phone and can play. This educational platform makes class material as fun as playing online trivia.

Socrative (https://www.socrative.com/)

When clickers are unavailable, students can use their cell phones as clickers. You create questions online, and students respond using their cell phones. Responses and trends can be seen in real time, and it can be used for games such as Jeopardy style reviews as well.

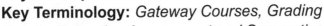

> **Key Concepts:** *Assessment*
> **Key Terminology:** *Gateway Courses, Grading Rubric, Formative Assessment and Summative Assessment*
> **Key Idea:** *There are many different assessment tools. Assessment needs to be relevant, engaging and appropriately measure learning.*

CHAPTER 8
LEARNING ASSESSMENT

We have covered a lot of information. In the last chapter, we discussed classroom strategies which create an active, student-centered learning environment. We have shared strategies to help you rethink your approaches to teaching. Now it is time to assess student mastery of course materials.

Student Accountability

In a blended and flipped course, students need to be held accountable for their learning. It is time to revisit your student learning outcomes. These have been your guide to creating a blended and flipped classroom. Review your learning outcomes to make sure they have been linked to your learning activities. Now you must determine whether students who have completed the course assignments and activities have mastered the skills and information needed to be successful in your course.

Assessment holds students accountable for the information they were expected to learn in your class. Learning activities must provide students with a roadmap to the information they need. If you have explored and perhaps even adapted the strategies in this book, you will already have assessed for mastery of facts by using a variety of learning strategies. Your classroom discussions will have helped your students synthesize the course content (higher level learning). Remember that simply because you are teaching using a flipped and blended format, this does not mean that the rigor of your class should be diminished. Maintain rigor as you design your assessments. This means your assessment of the unit or topic must allow students to demonstrate their knowledge on a higher level.

Where to Begin?

We will give you a list of unique, exciting assessment tools at the end of this chapter, but for now, let's begin the learning assessment process by focusing on your students. As you review your learning objectives, focus on the types of higher-level thinking from Bloom's Taxonomy: applying, analyzing, evaluating and creating.

If you teach in a discipline that has a directly-connected career (accounting, nursing or elementary education, i.e.), you will be well-acquainted with the learning and skills that are needed to be successful. Students need to know how to problem solve. They need to be well-versed in the qualitative analysis of information and data, or maybe they will need to know how to conduct an intake interview. Focusing on the necessary skills for a career-connected discipline will get you started on designing assessments which measure the level of student mastery in ways that will give your students real world practice.

If you teach in a discipline that is not directly related to a career, how will you design meaningful assessment tools? Focus on skills employers are looking for in college graduates. These skills will be broad: critical thinking, initiative, adaptability, teamwork, creativity and leadership. Such skills are always in demand, and you can help your students master them through your use of assessment.

Assessment— Much More Than Tests and Papers

Usually, when we think of assessment, we think of tests or research papers. These have been the go to, commonly accepted tools to measure learning, but are they the most effective assessment tools?

Assigning a research paper to students, especially students in gateway (introductory) courses can be problematic. The under-prepared student may wait until the last minute to throw together a substandard paper that does not demonstrate her/his level of understanding. In addition, students plagiarize, either on purpose or accidently, which sets them up for failure.

According to research by the International Center for Academic Integrity (ICAI), which has studied trends in academic dishonesty for more than a decade, about 68 percent of undergraduate students surveyed admit to cheating on tests or in written work. Forty-three percent of graduate students do the same (McCabe, 2015). Even more chilling is the fact that, according to McCabe, "....a diminishing level of student participation in his surveys—fewer responses, and fewer thoughtful responses. There's a growing apathy toward school and cheating at school among today's students" (*The Atlantic*, 2016).

While writing is an important skill to learn in college, crafting meaningful, relevant writing exercises is difficult and a significant portion of students may engage in academic dishonesty. Rethink your writing assignments in order to breathe new life into your course requirements and assessments.

One of the advantages of blended and flipped learning is that this platform makes the learning relevant and exciting. Learning and communication have been reorganized through the integration of technology. Assignments and assessment tools you can design for students in your blended and flipped classes can include allowing students to create videos, storyboards, podcasts and portfolios. These allow students to demonstrate their knowledge while practicing the skills needed for today's job market!

Technology has also dramatically increased the sheer amount of information available to you and your students. The information included in a research paper written for your course in the Fall may be outdated by the next semester. Students need to know how to find the most current information. Research papers afford students opportunities to learn to do that, but presenting information to work colleagues, for instance, is rarely done by preparing and sharing a research paper. Give students opportunities to present information in ways that help them strengthen the skills that today's employers value.

A final reason to rethink the term paper is purely a selfish one. If you create a dynamic alternative assessment tool, it will be a change from reading piles of papers. It opens the door for you to assess student mastery while you enjoy a variety of information presented in a variety of formats.

Now, let's talk tests and why you should rethink relying solely on them to assess whether your students understand the course materials. Unless you create an entirely new test each time you administer one, there is a good chance that your test questions are archived on the internet somewhere. Students can use technology to capture your test questions even if the test is administered in class. Most textbook publisher question banks are also available online. Every time a system gets created to limit cheating on tests, students find a way around it. When this happens, those tests merely measure how competently and quickly a student uses Google search tools.

Finally, papers and tests are only marginally connected to the skills that students will need in the workplace. Think of how the job market has changed over the last decade. From Uber drivers and app developers to sustainability managers and drone operators, jobs available today didn't exist a decade ago. The World Economics Forum estimates 65 percent of children entering primary school today will ultimately end up working in completely new job types that aren't on our radar yet (World Economics Forum, 2016). There is no reason to think that this trend is going to change. Therefore, while we need to teach students about our academic disciplines, we should also embrace other skills which our students will need when they enter a changing job market. What follows is a variety of ways to measure learning and student mastery.

Formative and Summative Assessments

Formative assessment is part of the instructional process. It is a tool to monitor student learning and to provide important feedback to the student. Use this type of assessment when designing the out-of-class assignments and during the in-class activities. Formative assessment has two critical functions. First, it allows the students to identify their weaknesses and helps them to determine what areas that they need to work on. Secondly, it allows you to identify problem areas in your teaching and course materials so that you can adjust them. Formative assessments should have some bearing on the course grade, but should generally be treated as low stakes with a lower point value and used as the learning is happening.

Summative assessment is used to measure student knowledge at certain times in the course, such as when finishing a unit of work. This measure is compared to a benchmark or standard, which is often set by your institution. Compared to formative assessment, summative assessment tends to have much higher stakes and higher point values. Summative assessment is a measure, and not necessarily a learning tool, whereas formative assessment is used more as a learning tool.

As we work through this chapter, the information will apply to both formative and summative assessment. The Faculty Innovation Center at the University of Texas, Austin (2017) offers several excellent methods of assessment.

Formative, Low-Stakes (Informal)

Written Reflections

Sometimes referred to as "Minute Papers" or "Muddiest Points," these popular assessment techniques have students reflect immediately following a learning opportunity (e.g., at the end of a class or after completing an out-of-class activity). Students are prompted to answer one or two basic questions such as:

"What was the most important thing you learned today?"

"What was the most confusing topic today?"

"What important question remains unanswered?"

Polls/Surveys

Data on student opinions, attitudes, behaviors or confidence in understanding can be gathered either during class (e.g., with a classroom response system) or outside of class. This can illustrate student engagement with the material as well as prior knowledge, misconceptions, and comprehension.

Checks for Understanding

Pausing every few minutes to see whether students are following along with the lesson not only identifies gaps in comprehension, but helps break up lectures (e.g., with Clicker questions) or online lessons (e.g., with embedded quiz questions) into more digestible bites.

Wrappers

"Wrapping" activities, using a set of reflective questions, can help students develop skills to monitor their own learning and adapt as necessary.

Formal Assessments

In-Class Activities

Having students work in pairs or small groups to solve problems creates space for powerful peer-to-peer learning and rich class discussion. Instructors and TAs can roam the classroom as students work, helping those who get stuck and guiding those who are headed in the wrong direction.

Quizzes

Gauge students' prior knowledge, assess progress midway through a unit, create friendly in-class competition, review before the test. Quizzes can be great tools that don't have to count heavily toward students' grades. Using quizzes to begin units is also a fun way to assess what your students already know, clear up misconceptions, and drive home the point of how much they will learn.

Online Learning Modules

Canvas and other Learning Management Systems allow students to solve problems or answer questions along the way. This can provide you with analytics on student responses and class performance in order to tailor your instruction to their particular learning needs.

Class Deliverables

In-class activities are designed so students, usually in groups, are required to submit a product of their work for a grade. Among the variety of techniques, the most effective will balance individual and group accountability and require students to think about authentic complex issues. Team-Based Learning uses the four S's in the design of collaborative application exercises: significant, same, specific, and simultaneous. Focusing on smaller details risks leaving gaps in student learning and may not address key learning objectives. The problems that students solve should be significant, that is, could students envision themselves being challenged? The best exercises typically are practice based and focused on major, overarching concepts.

Summative (High Stakes) Assessment

Summative assessment techniques evaluate student learning. These are high-stakes assessments (i.e., they have high point values) that occur at the end of an instructional unit or course and measure the extent to which students have achieved the desired learning outcomes.

Portfolios

Submitting a portfolio at the end of a course can be a powerful way for students to see the progress they have made. More than just a collection of students' work from the semester, good portfolios also include reflections on their learning. Asking students to spell out the concepts or techniques used with each piece, the themes addressed, and hurdles faced also brings a sense of completion to the learning process.

Videos, Podcasts, Projects, Presentations

These give students the chance to go deeper with the material to put the knowledge they have acquired to use or create something new from it. This level of application is an extremely important and often overlooked part of the learning process. These types of projects also give students who do not test well a chance to shine.

Exams

This includes mid-term exams, final exams, and tests at the end of course units. The best tests include several types of questions – short answer, multiple-choice, true-false, and short essay – to allow students to fully demonstrate what they know.

Student Self-Assessments

One way to assess student learning is to have students assess themselves. Assign reflective journal entries for students. A twist on this idea would be to have students complete a blog. You might require students to respond to other blogs with insights and ideas. You can create self-reports for students to complete that will help them measure themselves against a set level of mastery. All of these work well for formative assessment and can also be tweaked to use as summative assessments.

Research logs, lab reports and field notes can be used as either formative or summative assessments. Remember to provide detailed instructions and a sample of the outcome you expect. This will help students better understand what you require of them. If you are going to use any of these as a summative assessment, first allow the students to practice the skills you are requiring before giving them the assessment.

There are a variety of tools that students can complete to link different ideas together. Students can complete concept maps and Venn diagrams. This allows students to see the larger picture and how things are related. Again, these can be used for both summative and formative assessment. K-W-L charts are good for formative assessment—these are simply a paper that has been divided into 3 sections. In the first section, students list everything they know (K) about a topic. In the second section, students list the things that they want to (or need to) know about that topic (W), and in the final column, students list what they have learned (L).

You can have students prepare a "conference" presentation. This can be broken down into various pieces, including the proposal, research and writing an abstract. Each of these activities can make excellent formative assessments and the actual presentation can work well as the summative assessment. This activity allows students some variety in how they present their work. Some students may prefer to present a paper as their "conference" presentation while others might want to hold a roundtable or give a formal presentation.

Students can create a variety of products to showcase their knowledge. They can be required to write a chapter for a book, or a children's book, design a brochure or write a news article. With the technology that is available today, they can create a podcast, a public service announcement video or create an awareness campaign using their smart phones. Many LMS allow students to record and upload videos. Students can also design a Twitter campaign, create an Instagram account or even go to the Fakebook website, which is a fake Facebook website. Students can create Fakebook accounts and interact with each other. Websites like Piktochart allow students to create professional looking posters with a minimum of computer experience. If your students are not comfortable with technology, they can create posters the old fashioned way.

Portfolios are also a great way for students to gather information. You may require students to gather information on local agencies or businesses. This information can be compiled into a handbook for them to use in their profession. Websites like Padlet allow students to curate information electronically.

Service learning is another great way to give students hands-on experience. Service learning experiences can be coupled with blogs or journal entries to make them more measurable.

You can have students research and create programs to address issues covered in your classes. Have them research the issue, pick their audience and create a program to educate or inform. Allowing creativity in this process will increase student ownership of the project and will amaze you. We have had students write poetry, songs and give puppet shows just to name a few.

Case studies are another way to measure knowledge. You can curate the case studies yourself, or work with students to locate a news item that would be both relevant and appropriate. It is very easy to locate a news item and to have the students research it. Then students can examine it from various theories, identify where the problems are or offer solutions.

One final thought on assessment: You can have the students create the grading rubric themselves. This will increase buy in, and allow them some control over they project that they are working on.

Challenges

Generally, anytime a "new" teaching technique comes along, there is a good chance that it is going to be met with skepticism. While flipped and blended learning may appear to be new, it is largely a different application of tried and true teaching techniques. This is why you should keep your department chair in the loop as you integrate assessment techniques other than tests and papers. The more you dialogue with your chair, the more likely s/he will allow you to diverge from the norm. If you were to walk into the chair's office out of the blue and announce you no longer wanted to require the research paper that has been in the curriculum forever, your request is likely to be denied. Instead, by working with your chair, and demonstrating how your different assessment techniques are more effective, you are more likely to be supported, possibly even encouraged.

It may take more than convincing to make a change to the assessment tools used in your course. You may need to create the new assessment, use it along with the current forms of assessment and use the results to make your case. As long as you consistently show that your meaningful assessments are doing a credible job, you have a good chance of convincing your chair and any other administrators to permit their use.

Once you create unique, challenging assessments, you will need to make sure that students understand the requirements of the class. As long as the new assessments are well-crafted, relevant and engaging, the students should appreciate the deviation from the standard forms of assessment. The key is to link assessments to the learning objectives and necessary skills for the workplace.

All assessments are measurable—you can put a grade on them. A few ways to do that would include requiring a certain number of points that need to be made, use of a certain number of key words or requiring the work to be of a certain length. Once you decide how to measure success on these assessments, it is important to make sure that your instructions are clear and concise so that the students know what is expected of them. Creating a grading rubric will also be helpful for both the students and yourself. There are a variety of rubrics available online at Rubistar to help you get started or even provide you with a rubric that will work for you.

One final word on assessment. You will be assessing your students' learning at many points throughout the semester. You do not have to totally remove all tests or formal papers from the class. Many times departments and colleges may have assessment requirements. For example, many colleges require a formal final exam. You can combine these requirements with other forms of assessment. In addition, you may have some leeway in the creation of the mandatory elements, so you may be able to tweak them to better fit your needs. If you are required to complete a final exam, you can choose to make it a case study. Or if you have to have a paper, you might have the students compare and contrast how two different theories would look at a real life situation.

Technological Trip Ups

There are a variety of websites, apps and other technology available to help instructors create dynamic assessments. However, the truth is that not all students have the same level of knowledge, ability or access to technology. There are a few things that can be done to alleviate that problem. Take an inventory of the kinds of technology available to the students in your classroom. Create student groups so that every group has access to the required technology and at least one person who is able to use it.

As for using small groups, keep in mind that at commuter colleges, you may need to dedicate class time to group projects, since many commuter students have demanding lives and may not be able to meet with their group outside of class time. However, this is the beauty of flipped and blended classes; you can dedicate this time to these projects. In addition, because you are using class time, you, as the instructor, can have a more hands-on approach and guide the students as they work through the process.

If your campus has computer labs, you may be able to reserve the labs for some of your class meetings. This will ensure that all students have access to the technology required for the project. It will allow students to work either in groups or individually.

Finally, your campus library is a great resource. As you design your projects, communicate with one of the librarians. This helps them to understand the requirements of the project so that they are better able to help students who get stuck. It also allows them to share with you resources you may not have been aware of that can make your project even stronger. Collaboration is a key to making your flipped and blended assignments the best that they can be.

CHAPTER 9
MEASURING INSTRUCTOR SUCCESS

In the previous chapter, we discussed ways to assess student learning in your classes. Utilizing more than one method of measurement will help you more accurately ascertain the level of your students' comprehension. Once grades are calculated another very important question still needs to be addressed: *"How do I measure my own success?"*

Measuring The Success of Your Class

All too often, the success of a class, student and instructor are simply measured by the grades that the students have earned in the class. However, there are other kinds of information and data that need to be considered when measuring the success of a class: student engagement, student retention and instructor satisfaction also need to be considered.

Students who are engaged with the course materials stay in the class. "Student engagement in educationally purposeful activities during the first year of college had a positive, statistically significant effect on persistence, even after controlling for background characteristics, other college experiences during the first college year, academic achievement, and financial aid" (Kuh, Cruce, Shoup, Kinzie and Gonyea, 2008). Students who are engaged with course content learn the course content. These outcomes are strongly correlated with an active classroom. The flipped and blended course sets students up for success since flipping and blending allow for engaged, active learning.

Instructor satisfaction is another key in determining the success of your class. "Faculty are the linchpins to student success. They are at the center of student success not just as individual pieceworkers in increasingly large classrooms, but as a collective, engaged in various departmental and organizational initiatives to enhance student achievement" (Rhodes, 2012). Faculty matter in facilitating student engagement and success (Umbach and Wawrzynsky, 2005).

Instructors who create active learning course content will be more engaged with the course material. Why? The blended flipped classroom moves beyond the hour long "sage on the stage" lecture format and morphs it into a dynamic, challenging environment where course materials are created and analyzed (higher-level thinking goes on). The instructor is engaged, working alongside the students, creating and analyzing.

Final Grades

Do not get us wrong, summative [high-stakes] assessments are an important measure of student success. Grades are the measure by which students are expected to be judged. However, remember that final student grades as a measure of student success (and your success as an instructor) may not be perfect. We recommend including the students' final grades as part of your determination of how successful your class was, but not to rely solely on that measurement.

It's important to remember that you will have students who come to class prepared, ask excellent questions and engage you in conversations outside of the classroom. Such students may nonetheless do poorly on tests. Twenty percent of college students report suffering from test anxiety (American Test Anxiety Association, 2013). Therefore, if you only rely on grades as your assessment tool to gauge how you did as the course instructor, you won't capture the actual level of students' mastery (or your instructional skill). Use multiple assessment tools, and balance student grades against other forms of measurement.

Reflecting

One of the most important tasks you can do as an instructor is to spend time thinking about your class. You should be asking yourself questions such as, "Was that activity successful?" "How can I make that lesson stronger?" and "What is the best way to assess this learning?" These reflections should be ongoing as the semester and your course progress. Begin your reflections before the first class. If you have taught the class before, reflect on the activities and lessons that worked well and how your activities and lessons could be strengthened. If you have never taught before or have never taught the class, find out what other instructors are doing. Review course syllabi posted online. Talk to faculty who teach in your discipline and other disciplines as well.

It is important to think about the flow of the class as the semester progresses. Have the lessons built upon each other? Is the information being presented in a way that encourages students to make critical connections? It is better to make slight changes as you go along, than to wait until the end of the semester and realize that you did not achieve your goals and your students' outcomes were subpar.

We both have course assessment file folders we keep accessible all semester. As we teach, we add ideas, thoughts and keep a list of changes that need to be made to each course. It is an informal system that usually ends up being a bunch of pieces of scrap paper, including useful web site addresses that we have come across throughout the semester. Always make a notation on your notes to indicate which course and specific textbook chapter, activity, lesson or reading is most relevant to it. Jot down other quick thoughts and observations, as well. Obviously, the same file folder can exist digitally; your "notes" and observations can be kept conveniently in electronic format.

Before beginning to plan subsequent courses, that folder of ideas and reflections makes a reappearance as a resource. Reflecting on what did and didn't work as courses end, and having a quick source of new ideas, is a great way to constantly improve the course, student retention and success as well as improve your own engagement.

While reflection should begin even before you teach the class, it should also be ongoing throughout the semester. Before you begin each module, chapter or learning objective in your class, reflect on how you are going to teach it. Think about the learning outcomes you want and make sure that your activities, lessons, videos and readings support the outcomes.

Reflect after each class session, as well. Ask yourself questions such as: "Were my students engaged?" "Was I engaged?" and most importantly, "How can we make this class better?" We have found over the years that this is an important strategy in the blended and flipped type of learning. Not only should you brainstorm ways to make your lessons and materials more effective and engaging, you will also come up with alternative ways to deliver course content.

Those who have been teaching for a while know that each class has its own "personality." Because of the differences in class personalities, teaching is never a one size fits all affair. This is why having multiple ways to approach course content is important. For example, we have had classes populated with students who loved to work in groups and classes filled with students who preferred to work alone. Reflection and curation of ideas is an important step toward meeting the needs of your students and learning to leverage the "personalities" of your classes.

Student Surveys

"Having the opportunity to be a student in a very impressive flipped classroom semester-long group project, I will take the flexibility and humbleness that I've acquired with me into future internships and jobs. I got the chance to have a relationship with the students and teachers on a level above just coming to class and listening to a lecture. I will take these lessons learned and continue to grow in the future. For any students contemplating whether to take a flipped class or not, I would definitely say go for it. You have the opportunity to interact with your teachers and class members in such a fun way" (Perry, H., 2015).

An important part of this reflective process is to listen to your students. Sometimes you may conclude you are not reaching your students and have to focus on how to better engage them. Instead of groping around in the dark, trying to figure out how to find the right mix of activities for your classroom, distribute an anonymous survey to your students. Most LMS systems have this feature available, but if not hand out paper surveys in class and leave the room. Assign a student to collect them (to maintain anonymity of participants) and return them to you.

Remember that you are gathering information, not apologizing or laying blame for problems. Use this type of survey at the semester midpoint, even if the course is progressing well:

- It is a quick way to get feedback from the students;

- It can help you to avoid potential problems;

- It can help the students gain a feeling of control over their own education;

- It can bring to light new ideas or ways to approach course content.

One Minute Notes

These can be anonymous or you can require students to put their names on them. Ask a simple question the last five minutes of class and have the students write their answers to the prompt. You may ask students to identify three concepts or facts they learned, or to identify a course concept they are confused about. This gives you ongoing feedback about your class.

Student Evaluations

As you reflect on how well you achieved your goals, look at notes you made about the class as it was delivered. Look at student grades and think about the overall level of student engagement in class. In addition, look carefully at your student evaluations.

Most colleges offer end-of-class student evaluations for students to complete. Student evaluations incorporate closed-ended questions and some open-ended questions. The results are tabulated and emailed to the instructor, the department chair and the dean at the beginning of the following semester. We feel that student evaluations can be helpful in course planning in many ways.

Once the evaluations are deployed and available to our students, we spend class time explaining the importance of these evaluations. We emphasize the fact that they are anonymous and that we do not get the results until after final grades have been submitted. To further encourage participation, we make this an assignment, assigning a very small number of points to the activity. Because it is anonymous, we ask students to show us the screen that says that the evaluation has been submitted for the class. We also request that students tell us which activities they felt were helpful and which ones they felt were not on the surveys. We emphasize that changes are made to our classes based on their feedback.

One important point to remember is to not overuse survey instruments. If you overdo the surveys, students will stop taking them seriously. One survey in the middle of the semester and one at the end are usually about right. Use of the one minute notes can be done more often, even weekly. The important thing to remember is that you are asking your students to give you their time and effort. Be judicious of your requirements on their time. It is more important to engage with the subject matter than to answer repeated surveys. Finally, it is important to share the results of the survey with the students if you can. Explain the changes that will be made due to their input. Ask for clarification on anything you do not understand. Whatever you do, include the students in all steps of this process as much as you can.

Engagement (Yours and Theirs)

Reflecting on your engagement will reinvigorate your teaching. Lectures grow stale and memorized lectures rarely come from a place of passion. The weight of pulling students through a semester of coursework will wear down even the most enthusiastic faculty member. By flipping and blending our classes, we share the responsibility for learning with our students. Each class we teach offers the opportunity for innovation and critical thinking. Each class challenges us. This is exciting and allows us to share our love of our disciplines with our students on a whole new level.

Our increased engagement motivates us. This motivation helps us create classes that filled up quickly at our institution. Many of our students return to take other classes with us and they tell their friends to take classes with us. Blending and flipping allow us to maintain our passion for our work, and the students show their appreciation by signing up and completing our classes.

Student engagement is another aspect of your classroom performance that needs to be reflected upon. There are many ways that students show they are engaged. They come to class prepared to work. They ask questions and volunteer information in class. Of course not all students want to speak up in class. Make sure that you allow these students to engage in other ways. This could be through writing, audio recordings, videos or having an email or instant messaging conversation with the student about the course content.

After reflecting, analyze the data you have about your class. This includes final grades. If you taught this class before, do you see any changes in your final grades? In your flipped and blended course, expect an overall increase in final grades. Motivated students do better academically. How many students completed your class with average or below average grades? Identify the issues that may have contributed to poor student outcomes.

Examine your retention rates. How many students completed your class? Was there a point in the class when you lost multiple students? If so, what were you teaching at that point? Is there something you can do to make those parts of the class more user-friendly? Has your retention rate improved? How does your retention compare to department standards?

It is important to remember that teaching a blended and flipped course will require regular tweaking. You will regularly identify course materials, strategies, lesson plans and learning outcome goals that can be made stronger. New technology and world events will give you a constant stream of ideas that can be incorporated in your class. Just when you think you have your class in a really good place, your department will adopt a new textbook, and you will have to make necessary changes. There will always be new challenges. This is the nature of active learning and dynamic teaching.

While you are assessing your success, talk to others. Have a conversation with your chair or dean to verify that your courses and student outcomes are meeting the needs, goals and objectives of the department. Talk with others who teach. If you have a lesson that works really well, offer to share it. This type of sharing can open doors to a wide support network that can help you to be even more successful as you blend and flip your courses.

Visit your college's teaching and learning center. Particularly as an adjunct, it helps to seek out this resource. You may be surprised at what types of professional development are available to you. If you come from a small school, with limited resources, you may need to be a little more creative in your quest for support. Look at your professional organization to see if it offers any training that can help you. The more you learn about teaching and teaching methodology, the stronger you will be at your craft.

Keep in mind that teaching, no matter how skilled the instructor, is not always an amazing, perfect experience. There will be days when things go wrong. When this happens, take a bit of a break and try not to beat yourself up. Understand that everyone has a bad moment or a bad class. Treat such situations as opportunities to learn from your mistakes and mix-ups.

CHAPTER 10
EXPLORING OTHER USES FOR FLIPPED AND BLENDED COURSE TOOLS

Now What?

You now have a road map to begin flipping your classroom and blending your courses. We hope that you plan to give it a try. Creating a successful flipped and blended classroom requires your commitment to the process. Start small, but imagine big! How big can you imagine?

When we say imagine "big," we mean finding ways to make the flipped and blended classroom work to bring new ideas into reality. The flipped and blended classroom is not meant to be a way to simply add more course material to your syllabus. Yes, you will cover material more deeply in this type of classroom, but don't overload your students by adding additional complex topics for them to cover.

When we decided to flip and blend our courses, we did so over cups of coffee after a conference on flipped learning. Just as you may have done while reading our book, we realized we had been integrating parts of the flipped and blended method for years. We were both fans of active learning, and we realized we had been seeking a format that worked for us, and a name for what we wanted to do. But we didn't stop there.

Flipping and blending our respective sociology and psychology courses prompted us to consider a project we had both dreamed of having the time to do. Flipping allows face-to-face class time to be used for active learning, yet the students still receive the solid background of general information that they would get from a lecture. What to do with all of that extra class time sparked our imaginations. Projects may be simple or complex. For example, you can create an assignment that can be completed in a single class period, or commit fully to Project Based Learning (PBL) for an entire course. Project Based Learning is a teaching method in which students gain knowledge and skills by working for an extended period of time to investigate and respond to an authentic, engaging and complex question, problem, or challenge.

According to the Buck Institute of Education's Gold Standard PBL (http://www.bie.org/about/what_pbl), each project should include the following elements:

- Key Knowledge, Understanding, and Success Skills - The project is focused on student learning goals, including standards-based content and skills such as critical thinking/problem solving, collaboration, and self-management.

- Challenging Problem or Question - The project is framed by a meaningful problem to solve or a question to answer, at the appropriate level of challenge.

- Sustained Inquiry - Students engage in a rigorous, extended process of asking questions, finding resources, and applying information.

- Authenticity - The project features real-world context, tasks and tools, quality standards, or impact – or speaks to students' personal concerns, interests, and issues in their lives.

- Student Voice and Choice - Students make some decisions about the project, including how they work and what they create.

- Reflection - Students and teachers reflect on learning, the effectiveness of their inquiry and project activities, the quality of student work, obstacles and how to overcome them.

- Critique and Revision - Students give, receive and use feedback to improve their process and products.

- Public Product - Students make their project work public by explaining, displaying and/or presenting it to people beyond the classroom.

Whether you are truly using PBL or planning a smaller scale project for your course, these are good guidelines to use. The best part, though, is that using flipped and blended learning completely changes how you will approach projects with your students. Instead of having them work outside of the classroom with little or no direct guidance from you, you'll have the opportunity to work with them as they learn.

Consider This Setup:

1. Have students research outside of the classroom using both the basic knowledge you provide through out-of-class assignments and other resources.

2. Students then bring their research to class and either work individually or in groups to develop an outline of the project.

3. Meet with students in class to make sure they are on the right path, steer them in new directions, and gain formative assessment of their knowledge at different points in the process.

4. Students work in the classroom and seek assessment and guidance before committing themselves to their final plans.

5. Students then complete their work and present it in whatever manner you have chosen.

In a traditional classroom, the students would spend their time in class gaining knowledge, but there is rarely time for direct guidance on the deeper learning involved in a project. Can you imagine the greater depth possible when you are present in the process with them? Let's add another layer to this use of flipped and blended learning...collaboration. Collaboration has many forms. Let's first consider collaboration within the classroom.

Now that you have all of this time for active learning, and are considering projects, why not consider dividing the students in your course into teams to complete those projects?

The most extreme version of using teams is Team Based Learning (TBL). This is a type of flipped classroom that involves using teams (usually of 5-7 students) that are established at the beginning of the semester and remain together throughout the learning process. (Kaufman, 2003) Lessons are structured entirely around using teams to complete them, including out of class assignments, readiness assessments, and in class assignments.

TBL has an excellent efficacy track record. For example, in a 1998 study by Richard Hake, students taught using interactive methods achieved results nearly two standard deviations higher than students in a traditional classroom studying the same material. In 2004, Levine and colleagues employed TBL in a psychiatry clerkship and found that students in a TBL environment had a significantly higher pass rage on the national licensure exam. In 2010, Koles and colleagues not only found higher performance in their medical students, but showed stronger growth and improvement in the students who were the lowest achievers coming into the TBL program. An excellent source of information on TBL is the Team Based Learning Collaborative (www.teambasedlearning.org).

Though you do not have to use a fully-formed team based learning paradigm in your classroom, it is clear that collaboration between students is effective. Pairing that with the active learning that becomes possible in a flipped and blended classroom is a natural step. If this is something that you want to consider, keep these principles in mind:

1. Groups should be properly formed (e.g. Intellectual talent should be equally distributed). These teams are fixed for the whole course.

2. Students are accountable for their pre-learning and for teamwork.

3. Assignments must promote both learning and team development.

4. Students must receive frequent and immediate feedback (Team Based Learning Collaborative, 2017).

Collaboration does not have to remain contained in the classroom. Who on your campus might make a good collaborator? In our cases, we've explored several options...including each other.

Our introductory psychology and sociology students have enjoyed a collaborative project that we designed. For this project, we adopted the full semester option and chose to work together. We found common ground between our curricula, and designed a project that set teams which included students from both courses. We spent one in-class day each week in these mixed teams, each of us facilitating half of the teams. The students learned to utilize the research methods we were teaching to develop real solutions to real challenges on our campus. The capstone presentation was then opened to the entire faculty and staff, including the administration.

This was a large undertaking during its first cycle, but has gotten easier as we have continued to refine it. The students' feedback was overwhelmingly positive, as was the feedback from the faculty, staff and administrators who participated in the presentations. Our student retention during the first cycle was higher than the department and college average, and has been nearly 100 percent during subsequent cycles of the project. Even better, we have found that students who were enrolled with one of us for this collaborative course chose not only to continue into higher-level courses with their assigned instructor, but also to take courses with the co-instructor whenever possible. Several of the ideas developed by the student teams have been put into practice on our campus. It's a win/win!

A collaboration within the same department is easiest, and for an adjunct instructor the full-time faculty in your department are likely to be the most accessible to you. However, you can also use a collaborative project to get to know others on campus, and increase your own engagement. For example, how about having someone from the library work with your students on academic research? What professionals do you know in the workforce related to your field who might come in to judge your student projects or act as mentors for them? What charitable causes might give your students a direction for their projects and provide real-world application of their talents?

Librarians have had much success with flipping when it comes to library instruction sessions. A brief search of the published literature shows that flipping is gaining traction as a popular method of delivering and enhancing one-shot library sessions.

By Angela Davis

Flipped Instruction

It does take time and effort on the part of both the librarian and the instructor to coordinate, but the end result is well worth the time spent. My experience as an instruction librarian has been that students who have had some sort of exposure to the library's resources just prior to attending an in-person library session are more engaged, ask targeted questions, and are prepared for deeper learning. A flipped instruction model also gives the librarian the opportunity to create an active classroom learning experience. Successful library sessions are all about timing and point-of-need instruction, and flipping is an excellent means by which both the instructor and the librarian can create stimulating and meaningful classroom interactions.—*Angela Davis, Librarian, Pitt Community College, NC*

Teachers in a different department are also excellent partners, as are the counselors and professionals in the career services division. For example, one project undertaken in the introductory psychology courses is to work with the graphic design students on our community college campus to develop Mental Health Awareness Month posters and presentations. A collaboration in sociology between the introductory students and the counselors related to barriers students face to academic success has yielded valuable pamphlets to be shared with struggling students. Collaborations with the library career services has enabled students to see real applications of work they are doing in the classroom, as has involving mentors from related professions.

Teaching professionals speak of collaborations across courses that seem completely unrelated on the surface. Campus administrators are realizing the benefits of helping adjuncts to connect, through professional development opportunities and collaborative experiences, and this trend can only be beneficial.

If you truly want to "think big" when it comes to collaboration, why not consider a national or international collaboration in which your students work with students in a classroom across the country or across the world? With the technology available today (such as Skype, Google Hangouts, etc.) it's possible to open your mind and classroom to infinite learning opportunities.

As you ponder and plan your flipped and blended lesson or course, we hope that you find this book to be a useful tool. The bottom line in all of this discussion, though, is that flipped and blended learning creates possibility. Whether you start small or jump into the deep end as we did, commit to yourself to trying. We haven't regretted a second of our journey, and we know that you won't either.

Best wishes, and happy flipping!

COPYRIGHT FAIR USE GUIDELINES FOR COLLEGE FACULTY

Courtesy of the Stanford Copyright and Fair Use Center, Stanford University Libraries, Stanford University, 2017 (http://fairuse.stanford.edu/).

What Types of Creative Work Does Copyright Protect?

Copyright protects works such as poetry, movies, CD-ROMs, video games, videos, plays, paintings, sheet music, recorded music performances, novels, software code, sculptures, photographs, choreography and architectural designs.

To qualify for copyright protection, a work must be "fixed in a tangible medium of expression." This means that the work must exist in some physical form for at least some period of time, no matter how brief. Virtually any form of expression will qualify as a tangible medium, including a computer's random access memory (RAM), the recording media that capture all radio and television broadcasts, and the scribbled notes on the back of an envelope that contain the basis for an impromptu speech.

In addition, the work must be original — that is, independently created by the author. It doesn't matter if an author's creation is similar to existing works, or even if it is arguably lacking in quality, ingenuity or aesthetic merit. So long as the author toils without copying from someone else, the results are protected by copyright.

Permission: What Is It and Why Do I Need It?

Obtaining copyright permission is the process of getting consent from a copyright owner to use the owner's creative material. Obtaining permission is often called "licensing"; when you have permission, you have a license to use the work. Permission is often (but not always) required because of intellectual property laws that protect creative works such as text, artwork, or music. (These laws are explained in more detail in the next section.) If you use a copyrighted work without the appropriate permission, you may be violating—or "infringing"—the owner's rights to that work. Infringing someone else's copyright may subject you to legal action. As if going to court weren't bad enough, you could be forced to stop using the work or pay money damages to the copyright owner.

As noted above, permission is not always required. In some situations, you can reproduce a photograph, a song, or text without a license. Generally, this will be true if the work has fallen into the public domain, or if your use qualifies as what's called a "fair use." Both of these legal concepts involve quite specific rules. In most cases, however, permission is required, so it is important to never assume that it is okay to use a work without permission.

Many people operate illegally, either intentionally or through ignorance. They use other people's work and never seek consent. This may work well for those who fly under the radar—that is, if copyright owners never learn of the use, or don't care enough to take action.

Obtaining Clearance for Coursepacks

It is the instructor's obligation to obtain clearance for materials used in class. Instructors typically delegate this task to one of the following:

*   Clearance services. These services are the easiest method of clearance and assembly.

*   University bookstores or copy shops. University policies may require that the instructor delegate the task to the campus bookstore, copy shop, or to a special division of the university that specializes in clearances.

Using a Clearance Service

It can be time-consuming to seek and obtain permission for the 20, 30, or more articles you want to use in a coursepack. Fortunately, private clearance services will, for a fee, acquire permission and assemble coursepacks on your behalf. After the coursepacks are created and sold, the clearance service collects royalties and distributes the payments to the rights holders. Educational institutions may require that the instructor use a specific clearance service.

The largest copyright clearing service is the Copyright Clearance Center (www.copyright.com), which clears millions of works from thousands of publishers and authors.

In 2001, XanEdu (www.xanedu.com), acquired the coursepack service formerly known as Campus Custom Publishing. In addition to providing traditional coursepack assembly, XanEdu offers an electronic online service that provides supplemental college course materials directly to the instructor's desktop via the internet.

Educational Uses of Non-Coursepack Materials

Unlike academic coursepacks, other copyrighted materials can be used without permission in certain educational circumstances under copyright law or as a fair use. "Fair use" is the right to use portions of copyrighted materials without permission for purposes of education, commentary or parody.

The Code of Best Practices in Fair Use for Media Literacy Education

In 2008, the Center for Media and Social Impact, in connection with American University, unveiled a guide of fair use practices for instructors in K–12 education, in higher education, in nonprofit organizations that offer programs for children and youth, and in adult education. The guide identifies five principles that represent acceptable practices for the fair use of copyrighted materials. You can learn more at the center's website, (www.cmsimpact.org).

Guidelines Establish a Minimum, Not a Maximum

In a case alleging 75 instances of infringement in an educational setting, 70 instances were not infringing because of fair use and for other reasons. The infringements were alleged because of the posting of copyrighted books within a university's e-reserve system. The court viewed the Copyright Office's 1976 Guidelines for Educational Fair Use as a minimum, not a maximum standard. The court then proposed its own fair use standard—10% of a book with less than ten chapters, or of a book that is not divided into chapters, or no more than one chapter or its equivalent in a book of more than ten chapters.—*Cambridge University Press v. Georgia State University*, Case 1:08-cv-01425-OD (N.D. Ga., May 11, 2012).

What is the Difference Between the Guidelines and Fair Use Principles?

The educational guidelines are similar to a treaty that has been adopted by copyright owners and academics. Under this arrangement, copyright owners will permit uses that are outlined in the guidelines. In other fair use situations, the only way to prove that a use is permitted is to submit the matter to court or arbitration. In other words, in order to avoid lawsuits, the various parties have agreed on what is permissible for educational uses, codified in these guidelines.

What is an "Educational Use?"

The educational fair use guidelines apply to material used in educational institutions and for educational purposes. Examples of "educational institutions" include K-12 schools, colleges, and universities. Libraries, museums, hospitals, and other nonprofit institutions also are considered educational institutions under most educational fair use guidelines when they engage in nonprofit instructional, research, or scholarly activities for educational purposes.

"Educational Purposes" are:

- noncommercial instruction or curriculum-based teaching by educators to students at nonprofit educational institutions

- planned noncommercial study or investigation directed toward making a contribution to a field of knowledge, or

- presentation of research findings at noncommercial peer conferences, workshops, or seminars.

Rules for Reproducing Text Materials for Use in Class

The guidelines permit a teacher to make one copy of any of the following: a chapter from a book; an article from a periodical or newspaper; a short story, short essay, or short poem; a chart, graph, diagram, drawing, cartoon, or picture from a book, periodical, or newspaper.

Teachers may not photocopy workbooks, texts, standardized tests, or other materials that were created for educational use. The guidelines were not intended to allow teachers to usurp the profits of educational publishers. In other words, educational publishers do not consider it a fair use if the copying provides replacements or substitutes for the purchase of books, reprints, periodicals, tests, workbooks, anthologies, compilations, or collective works.

Rules for Reproducing Music

A music instructor can make copies of excerpts of sheet music or other printed works, provided that the excerpts do not constitute a "performable unit," such as a whole song, section, movement, or aria. In no case can more than 10% of the whole work be copied and the number of copies may not exceed one copy per pupil. Printed copies that have been purchased may be edited or simplified provided that the fundamental character of the work is not distorted or the lyrics altered.

A student may make a single recording of a performance of copyrighted music for evaluation or rehearsal purposes, and the educational institution or individual teacher may keep a copy. In addition, a single copy of a sound recording owned by an educational institution or an individual teacher (such as a tape, disc, or cassette) of copyrighted music may be made for the purpose of constructing aural exercises or examinations, and the educational institution or individual teacher can keep a copy.

Rules for Recording and Showing Television Programs

Nonprofit educational institutions can record television programs transmitted by network television and cable stations. The institution can keep the tape for 45 days, but can only use it for instructional purposes during the first ten of the 45 days. After the first ten days, the video recording can only be used for teacher evaluation purposes, to determine whether or not to include the broadcast program in the teaching curriculum. If the teacher wants to keep it within the curriculum, he or she must obtain permission from the copyright owner. The recording may be played once by each individual teacher in the course of related teaching activities in classrooms and similar places devoted to instruction (including formalized home instruction). The recorded program can be repeated once if necessary, although there are no standards for determining what is and is not necessary. After 45 days, the recording must be erased or destroyed.

A video recording of a broadcast can be made only at the request of and only used by individual teachers. A television show may not be regularly recorded in anticipation of requests—for example, a teacher cannot make a standing request to record each episode of a PBS series. Only enough copies may be reproduced from each recording to meet the needs of teachers, and the recordings may not be combined to create teaching compilations. All copies of a recording must include the copyright notice on the broadcast program as recorded and (as mentioned above) must be erased or destroyed after 45 days.

References

7 Things You Should Know About Flipped Classrooms. EDUCAUSE Learning Initiative (ELI) Collection(s): Feb. 2012, https://library.educause.edu/resources/2012/2/7-things-you-should-know-about-flipped-classrooms.

7 Things You Should Know About Flipped Learning. [ebook] Educause, 2012. https://library.educause.edu/~/media/files/library/2012/2/eli7081-pdf.pdf.

American Test Anxiety Association, http://amtaa.org/.

Anderson, Karen, and Frances A. May. "Does the Method of Instruction Matter? An Experimental Examination of Information Literacy Instruction in the Online, Blended, and Face-to-Face Classrooms." The Journal of Academic Librarianship, vol. 36, no. 6, 2010, pp. 495–500., doi:10.1016/j.acalib.2010.08.005.

Anderson, Lorin W., et al. A Taxonomy for Learning, Teaching, and Assessing: a Revision of Bloom's Taxonomy of Educational Objectives: Complete Edition. New York, Longman, 2001.

Armstrong, Scott J. "Natural Learning in Higher Education," Encyclopedia of the Sciences of Learning, 2012.

Association of American Colleges and Universities, 2010.

Austin, Diane, and Nadine Mescia. "Strategies to Incorporate Active Learning into Online." International Conference on Technology and Education, 2001.

Barkley, Elizabeth F., et al. Collaborative Learning Techniques: a Handbook for College Faculty. San Francisco, CA, Jossey-Bass, A Wiley Brand, 2014.

Barthel, Margaret. "How to Stop Cheating in College." The Atlantic, April, 2016.

Barnes, Douglas R. Active Learning. Leeds, UK, Leeds University TVEI Support Project, 1989.

Barnes and Noble College Insights, 2016. "Achieving Success for Non-Traditional Students." https://www.bncollege.com/Achieving-Success-for-Non-Traditional-Students-01-11-17.pdf

Beck, Evelyn, and Donald Greive. Going the Distance: a Handbook for Part-Time & Adjunct Faculty Who Teach Online. Ann Arbor, MI, The Part-Time Press, Inc., 2005.

Bhagat, Kaushal Kumar, et al. "The Impact Of The Flipped Classroom On Mathematics Concept Learning In High School." Journal Of Educational Technology & Society, vol. 19.3, 2016, pp. 134–142.

Bligh, Donald A. What's the Use of Lectures? San Francisco, CA, Jossey-Bass, 2000

"Bloom's Taxonomy." Vanderbilt University Center for Teaching, cft. vanderbilt.edu/guides-sub-pages/blooms-taxonomy/.

Boeren, Ellen. "The Blended Learning Environment in Higher Education:" Blended Learning: Concepts, Methodologies, Tools, and Applications, pp. 252–270.

Britton, Bruce K., and Abraham Tesser. "Effects of Time-Management Practices on College Grades." Journal of Educational Psychology, vol. 83, no. 3, 1991, pp. 405–410.

Buck Institute of Education's Gold Standard PBL. April 2015, (http://www.bie.org/about/what_pbl).

Christenson, Sandra, et al. Handbook of Research on Student Engagement. New York, Springer, 2012.

Connell, N., Klem, J. "Narrative approaches to the transfer of organisational knowledge," Knowledge Management Research & Practice, December 2004, Volume 2, Issue 3, pp 184–193.

Crappell, Courtney. "The ABCs of Gen X, Y(P), Z: Dealing with Millennial Parents: A Column for Young Professionals." American Music Teacher, 1 Dec. 2015, pp. 40–43.

Eisenberg, Daniel, et al. "Mental Health and Academic Success in College." The B.E. Journal of Economic Analysis & Policy, vol. 9, no. 1, 2009, doi:10.2202/1935-1682.2191.

Eryilmaz, Meltem. "The Effectiveness Of Blended Learning Environments." Contemporary Issues in Education Research (CIER), vol. 8, no. 4, Feb. 2015, p. 251., doi:10.19030/cier.v8i4.9433.

"Framework for Campus Mental Health Promotion and Suicide Prevention." SAMHSA Campus Suicide Prevention Grantee

Technical Assistance Meeting, 2007.

Francescucci, Anthony, and Mary Foster. "The VIRI (Virtual, Inter-active, Real-Time, Instructor-Led) Classroom: The Impact of Blended Synchronous Online Courses on Student Performance, Engagement, and Satisfaction." The Canadian Journal of Higher Education, vol. 43, no. 3, 2013, pp. 78–91.

Gabriel, Kathleen F. Teaching Unprepared Students: Strategies for Promoting Success and Retention in Higher Education. Sterling, VA, Stylus, 2008.

"Getting to Know Gen Z: Exploring a New Generation's Expecta-tions for Higher Education." Nov. 2015, next.bncollege.com/wp-content/uploads/2015/10/Gen-Z-Research-Report-Final.pdf.

Greenfield, R. 2013. "The Internet's Attention Span for Video Is Quickly Shrinking." The Atlantic, August, 2013.

Greive, Donald. Handbook II: Advanced Teaching Strategies for Adjunct and Part-Time Faculty, 3rd ed., Ann Arbor, MI, Part-Time Press, 2016.

Greive, Donald. Teaching Strategies & Techniques for Adjunct Faculty. Ann Arbor, MI, Part-Time Press, 2009.

Greive, Donald, and Patricia Lesko. A Handbook for Adjunct/Part-Time Faculty and Teachers of Adults. 7th ed., Ann Arbor, MI, The Part-Time Press, 2011.

Gruttadaro, Darcy, and Dana Crudo. "College Students Speak: A Survey Report on Mental Health." NAMI: National Alliance on Mental Illness, NAMI: National Alliance on Mental Illness, 2012, www.nami.org/namioncampus.

Hake, Richard R. "Interactive-Engagement versus Traditional Meth-ods: A Six-Thousand-Student Survey of Mechanics Test Data for Introductory Physics Courses." American Journal of Physics, vol. 66, no. 1, 1998, pp. 64–74.

Hainline, Louise, et. al. "Changing Students, Faculty, and Institutions in the Twenty-First Century." Association of American Colleges & Universities, Peer Review, Summer 2010, Vol. 12, No. 3..

Hansen, Randall. "College Professor Pet-Peeves." Quintessential, www.livecareer.com/quintessential/college-professor-pet-peeves. Accessed 7 May 2017.

Hill, Bonnie Campbell, et al. Classroom Based Assessment. Norwood, MA, Christopher-Gordon Publishers, 1998.

Honeycutt, B. 2016. "Five Ways to Motivate Unprepared Students in the Flipped Classroom." Faculty Focus, April 4, 2016.

Hsiao, Karin Petersen. "First-Generation College Students." (ERIC ED351079) ERIC Digest, November, 1992. Office of Educational Research and Improvement. Los Angeles, CA: ERIC Clearinghouse Products (071). www.eric.ed.gov

Kaufman, D. M. "ABC of Learning and Teaching in Medicine: Applying Educational Theory in Practice." Bmj, vol. 326, no. 7382, 2003, pp. 213–216., doi:10.1136/bmj.326.7382.213.

Kessler, Ronald C., et al. "Lifetime Prevalence and Age-of-Onset Distributions of DSM-IV Disorders in the National Comorbidity Survey Replication." Archives of General Psychiatry, vol. 62, no. 6, Jan. 2005, p. 593., doi:10.1001/archpsyc.62.6.593.

Kessler, Ronald C., et al. "Prevalence, Severity, and Comorbidity of 12-Month DSM-IV Disorders in the National Comorbidity Survey Replication." Archives of General Psychiatry, vol. 62, no. 6, Jan. 2005, p. 617., doi:10.1001/archpsyc.62.6.617.

Kisch, Jeremy, et al. "Aspects of Suicidal Behavior, Depression, and Treatment in College Students: Results from the Spring 2000 National College Health Assessment Survey." Suicide and Life-Threatening Behavior, vol. 35, no. 1, 2005, pp. 3–13.

Klem, Adena M.; Connell, James P. "Relationships Matter: Linking Teacher Support to Student Engagement and Achievement." Journal of School Health, vol. 74 no. 7, Sept. 2004, pp. 262-273.

Koles, Paul G., et al. "The Impact of Team-Based Learning on Medical StudentsÊ¼ Academic Performance." Academic Medicine, vol. 85, no. 11, 2010, pp. 1739–1745., doi:10.1097/acm.0b013e3181f52bed.

Kraushaar, J. & Novak, D. "Examining the Effects of Student Multi-tasking with Laptops During the Lecture." Journal of Information Systems Education, 2010, vol. 21(2).

Krupnick, Matt. "Colleges Respond to Growing Ranks of Learning Disabled." The Hechinger Report, The Hechinger Report, 12 Feb. 2015, hechingerreport.org/colleges-respond-to-growing-ranks-of-learning-disabled/.

Kuh, George D., Cruce, Ty M., Shoup, Rick, Kinzie, Jillian, Gonyea, Robert M. "Unmasking the Effects of Student Engagement on First-Year College Grades and Persistence." The Journal of Higher Education, Vol. 79, No. 5 (Sep. - Oct., 2008), pp. 540-563.

LaVergne, Debra Kaye. "Blended Learning in Higher Education: Comparison of Faculty and Student Attitudes Regarding Course Effectiveness."

Leach, Linda, Zepke, Nick. "Improving student engagement: Ten proposals for action." Active Learning in Higher Education, October 26, 2010.

Levine, Ruth E., et al. "Transforming a Clinical Clerkship with Team Learning." Teaching and Learning in Medicine, vol. 16, no. 3, 2004, pp. 270–275., doi:10.1207/s15328015tlm1603_9.

McCabe, Donald. International Center for Academic Integrity. http://www.academicintegrity.org/icai/integrity-3.php, 2015.

McCrindle, Mark (2015). "The McCrindle Blog: The Generation Map." [online] Available at: http://mccrindle.com.au/resources/whitepapers/McCrindle-Research_ABC-03_The-Generation-Map_Mark-McCrindle.pdf.

Means, Barara, et al. "The Effectiveness of Online and Blended Learning: A Meta-Analysis of the Empirical Literature." Teachers College Record, vol. 115, Mar. 2013.

"Methods of Assessment." Faculty Innovation Center, The University of Texas at Austin, 2016-2017. https://facultyinnovate.utexas.edu/teaching/check-learning/methods.

Mitchell, Anthony, and Sue Honore. "Criteria for Successful Blended Learning." Industrial and Commercial Training, vol. 39, no. 3, 2007, pp. 143–149.

Mitchell, K. "Making the grade: Help and hope for the first-generation college student." ERIC Review, 5, (3), 13-15. (ED 413 886).

Mok, Heng Ngee. " Teaching Tip: The Flipped Classroom." Journal of Information Systems Education, vol. 25, no. 1, 2014, pp. 7–11.

Mott, Jennifer, and Steffen Peuker. "Using Team-Based Learning to Ensure Student Accountability and Engagement in Flipped Classrooms." 2015 ASEE Annual Conference and Exposition Proceedings, doi:10.18260/p.25022.

Newmann, F. M., Wehlage, G. G. & Lamborn, S. D.. The significance and sources of student engagement. In F. Newmann (Ed.), Student engagement and achievement in American secondary schools. New York: Teachers College Press, 1993.

Nilson, Linda B. Teaching at Its Best: a Research-Based Resource for College Instructors. San Franciso, Jossey-Bass, 2016.

"NMC Horizon Report > 2017 Higher Education Edition." The New Media Consortium, 2017, www.nmc.org/publication/nmc-horizon-report-2017-higher-education-edition/.

Novotney, Amy. "Students under pressure." Monitor on Psychology, September 2014, Vol 45, No. 8.

Nwosisi, Christopher, et al. "A Study of the Flipped Classroom and Its Effectiveness in Flipping Thirty Percent of the Course Content." International Journal of Information and Education Technology, vol. 6, no. 5, 2016, pp. 348–351., doi:10.7763/ijiet.2016.v6.712.

Opidee, Ioanna. "Supporting First-Gen College Students." University Business Magazine, University Business, Feb. 2015, www.universitybusiness.com/article/supporting-first-gen-college-students.

"Overview." Team-Based Learning Collaborative, Team-Based Learning Collaborative, 2017, www.teambasedlearning.org/definition/.

Pastorino, Ellen. "Traditionalists, Baby Boomers, Gen X'Ers, and Millennials in the Classroom: When Generations Collide." PsycEXTRA Dataset.

"Percentage Distribution of U.S. Resident Undergraduate Enrollment in Degree-Granting Postsecondary Institutions, by Institutional Level and Control and Student Race/Ethnicity: Fall 2014." National Center for Educational Statistics, U.S. Department of Education, National Center for Education Statistics, Integrated Postsecondary Education Data System (IPEDS), 2014.

"Percentage of Full-Time Undergraduate Enrollment in Degree-Granting Postsecondary Institutions, by Institutional Level and Control and Student Age: Fall 2013." National Center for Educational Statistics, U.S. Department of Education, National Center for Education Statistics, Integrated Postsecondary Education Data ;Eve;SSystem (IPEDS), 2014, nces.ed.gov/programs/coe/indicator_csb.asp#info.

Perry, Hali. Excerpt from "Flipped Classroom Post-project Student Reflection," Pitt Community College, Spring 2015.

Petty, Tanjula. "Motivating First-Generation Students to Academic Success." College Student Journal, vol. 448, no. 2, 2014, pp. 257–264.

Pohl, Michael. Learning to Think, Thinking to Learn: Models and Strategies to Develop a Classooom Culture of Thinking. Cheltenham, Victoria, Australia, Hawker Brownlow Education, 2000.

Poon, Joanna. "Use of Blended Learning to Enhance the Student Learning Experience and Engagement in Property Education." Property Management, vol. 30, no. 2, June 2012, pp. 129–156.

Provitera-McGlynn, Angela. Successful Beginnings for College Teaching Engaging Your Students from the First Day. Madison, WI, Atwood Publ., 2001.

"Revised Bloom's Taxonomy." Revised Bloom's Taxonomy, http://www.kurwongbss.qld.edu.au/thinking/Bloom/blooms.htm.

Rhodes, Gary. "Faculty Engagement to Enhance Student Attainment." Paper prepared for National Commission on Higher Education Attainment, 2012, http://www.acenet.edu/news-room/Documents/Faculty-Engagement-to-Enhance-Student-Attainment--Rhoades.pdf.

Ryan, Sarah, et al. "The Effectiveness of Blended Online Learning Courses at the Community College Level." Community College Journal of Research and Practice, vol. 40, no. 4, Nov. 2015, pp. 285–298.

Sadik, Alaa. "14th European Conference on e-Learning ECEL-2015." The Effectiveness of Flipped Lectures in Improving Student Engagement and Satisfaction, 2015.

Sen, Tushar Kanti. "Application of Blended and Traditional Class Teaching Approach in Higher Education and the Student Learining Experience." International Journal of Innovation, Management and Technology, vol. 2, no. 2, Apr. 2011, pp. 107–109.

Sun, Jerry Chih-Yuan, and Yu-Ting Wu. "Analysis of Learning Achievement and Teacher-Student Interactions in Flipped and Conventional Classrooms." The International Review of Research in Open and Distributed Learning, vol. 17, no. 1, Feb. 2016.

"The Six Living Generations in America." The Six Living Generations In America, www.marketingteacher.com/the-six-living-generations-in-america/.

Smith, Jay P. "The Efficacy of a Flipped Learning Classroom." McKendree University , 2015.

Stanford Copyright and Fair Use Center, Stanford University Libraries, Stanfold University, 2017, (http://fairuse.stanford.edu/).

Taylor, J. (2010). From Baby Boomers to Generation Alpha: The ScribbleLive Guide to Generational Marketing - ScribbleLive. [online] ScribbleLive. Available at: http://www.scribblelive.com/blog/2015/10/09/baby-boomers-generation-alpha-scribblelive-guide-generational-marketing/

Thibodeaux, J., Deutsch, A., Kitsantas, A., Winsler, A. "First-Year College Students' Time Use: Relations With Self-Regulation and GPA." Journal of Advanced Academics, 28 (1), 5-27, 2016.

Umbach, Paul, and Wawrzynsky, M. 2005. "Faculty do matter: The role of college faculty in student learning and engagement." Research in Higher Education, 46,2:153-84.

University of Minnesota Center for Educational Innovation. "Active Learning Classrooms | Center For Educational Innovation," 2017. https://cei.umn.edu/support-services/tutorials/active-learning-classrooms.

Webb, Michael, Mayka, Liz. "Unconventional Wisdom: A Profile of the Graduates of Early College High School." Jobs for the Future, Mar. 2011, www.jff.org/publications/unconventional-wisdom-profile-graduates-early-college-high-school.

Westermann, Edward B. "A Half-Flipped Classroom or an Alternative Approach?: Primary Sources and Blended Learning." Educational Research Quarterly, vol. 38, no. 2, Dec. 2014, pp. 43–57.

"What Is Project Based Learning (PBL)?" What Is PBL? | Project Based Learning | BIE, Buck Institute for Education, www.bie.org/about/what_pbl.

White, S., Olenick, B., and Bray, T. "College students on the autism spectrum: prevalence and associated problems." Autism, 2011, Nov;15(6):683-701.

Wiedmer, Terry. "Generations Do Differ: Best Practices in Leading Traditionalists, Boomers, and Generations x, y, and z." The Delta Kappa Gamma Bulletin: International Journal for Professional Educators, vol. 82, no. 1, 2015, pp. 51–58.

Winstead, S. "7 Technical Tips for Creating Video Lectures." elearningbrothers.com, June, 2016. Retrieved June 6, 2017 from the World Wide Web: http://elearningbrothers.com/7-technical-tips-for-creating-video-lectures/.

Wong, Lily, et al. "A Framework for Investigating Blended Learning Effectiveness." Education Training, vol. 56, no. 2/3, Aug. 2014, pp. 233–251.

World Economic Forum. "Human Capital Outlook." http://www3.weforum.org/docs/WEF_ASEAN_HumanCapitalOutlook.pdf. 2016.

Zepke, Nick, and Linda Leach. "Improving Student Engagement: Ten Proposals for Action." Active Learning in Higher Education, vol. 11, no. 3, 2010, pp. 167–177.

Index

C

D

E

Mitchell, K. 43
Monopoly 87
Moodle. *See* learning management system
muddy point 33
multi-media 24, 28

N

National Alliance on Mental Illness 49
National Center for Educational Statistics 44
NCCCSPA. *See* North Carolina Community College Sociology and
Psychology Association
Newman, F.M. 26
New Media Consortium Horizon Report 41
non-traditional students 126
North Carolina Community College Sociology and Psychology Association
11
North Carolina Wesleyan University 59
Norton. *See* virus protection
Novak, D. 47, 48, 130
Novotney, A. 43

O

Oates, Sadie 11
Olenick, B. 43
One Minute Notes 6, 109. *See also* assessment
online lecture 73
Open Office. *See* software
OpenStax. *See* publisher content
Opidee, J. 43
Orndorf, Porscha 8

P

Padlet 101
Part-Time Press 144
PBL. *See* Project Based Learning
PBS 125
PC Magazine 55
pedagogy 7, 17, 20, 23, 24, 30, 41, 67, 68
Perry, H. 108
pet peeves 13, 14, 85
Piktochart 101
Pitt Community College 16, 31, 118
plagiarism 63
Plickers 91
podcasts 6, 99
portfolio 99
PowerPoint 34, 56, 65, 74, 91
PowerPoint Office Mix. *See* screencasting
Preast, Lori 11
preparation 28, 52, 57, 65, 68, 78, 84, 85, 87, 88
presentations 10, 29, 31, 35, 72, 76, 91, 117, 118
problem-based learning 35
professional development 31, 51, 67, 112, 119
Project Based Learning 113, 114
publisher content 73

If you found this book helpful, you'll want to check out these other titles:

A Handbook for Adjunct/Part-Time Faculty and Teachers of Adults, 7th ed. **by Donald Greive and P.D. Lesko**

With over 265,000 copies sold, *A Handbook* is one of the most trusted faculty development resources available today. *A Handbook* offers practical advice and successful strategies in a readable, accessible style and format. This powerhouse helps readers tackle the day-to-day challenges associated with teaching part-time. The book takes faculty (including those new to the classroom) step-by-step through the semester. Readers begin with a discussion about the importance of andragogy, student-centered learning and cooperative/collaborative learning. The book offers suggestions, teaching tips and helps instructors sharpen their skills in order to become more confident and competent in the classroom. *A Handbook* helps readers build stronger lessons plans, integrate media and technology into lectures effectively, facilitate more dynamic classroom discussions and craft a variety of test types and assessment tools (including self-assessment tools). Available in paperback for $20.00 per copy.

Going the Distance: A Handbook for Adjunct & Part-Time Faculty Who Teach Online, Revised 1st Edition **by Evelyn Beck and Donald Greive, Ed.D.**

Whether you're just thinking about teaching online, a first-time online course facilitator, or you are an experienced distance educator, *Going the Distance: A Handbook for Part-Time & Adjunct Faculty Who Teach Online* will help you sharpen your online teaching skills, develop and deliver more richly-structured distance education courses. The revised edition contains updated and expanded sections on student retention, technology, distance learning conferences, awards & fellowships, and course development. *Going the Distance* is available in paperback for $15.00. Also available as a set with *A Handbook for Adjunct/Part-Time Faculty and Teachers of Adults, 7th ed.*, $30.00/set.

FAQ's...

How can I place an orders?

Orders can be placed **by mail** to Part-Time Press, P.O. Box 130117, Ann Arbor, MI 48113-0117, **by phone/fax** at (734)930-6854, and **online** at http://www.Part-TimePress.com.

How much do I pay if I order multiple copies?

Part-Time Press books have a quantity discount schedule available:

10-49 copies—10% discount
50-99 copies— 20% discount
100 or more copies—30% discount

How can I pay for orders?

Orders can be placed with **a purchase order** or can be paid by **check**, **PayPal** or **credit card** (Visa/Mastercard, Discover or AMEX.)

How will my order be shipped?

Standard shipping to a continental U.S. street address is via **UPS-Ground Service**. Foreign shipments or U.S. post office box addresses go through the **U.S. Postal Service** and express shipments via **UPS-2nd Day**, or **UPS-Next Day**. Shipping and handling charges are based on the dollar amount of the shipment, and a fee schedule is shown on the next page.

What if I'm a reseller like a bookstore or wholesaler?

Resellers get a standard **20% discount** off of the single copy retail price, or may choose to receive the multiple copy discount.

Part-Time Press Books: Order Form

Qty	Title	Unit $$	Total
	Blended Learning and Flipped Classrooms, 1st ed.	**$20.00**	
	Handbook II: Advanced Teaching Strategies	**$20.00**	
	Going the Distance: A Handbook for Part-Time & Adjunct Faculty Who Teach Online, Rev. 1st ed.	**$15.00**	
	Teaching in the Sciences	**$20.00**	
	Getting Down to Business	**$20.00**	
	Teaching Strategies and Techniques, 5th ed.	**$15.00**	
	Teaching & Learning in College	**$20.00**	
	The Undergrad Library Collection (7 book collection)	**$115.00**	
	Handbook for Adjunct/Part-Time Faculty, 7th ed.	**$20.00**	
		Subtotal	
		Shipping	

Shipping Schedule:

1-4 books $6.00

5+ books   8 percent of the purchase price

Part-Time Press: P.O. Box 130117, Ann Arbor, MI 48113-0117
Fax/Phone: 734-930-6854 Email: orders@part-timepress.com
Order securely online: http://www.Part-TimePress.com
Canadian customers order securely online: http://ca.part-timepress.com

Purchaser/Payment Information

☐ Check (payable to The Part-Time Press)
☐ Credit Card # _____   Exp._____
     CVV# _____
☐ Purchase Order # _____
Name _____
Institution _____
Address _____ City/ST/Zip _____
Ph:_____ Email: _____